GENES
&DNA

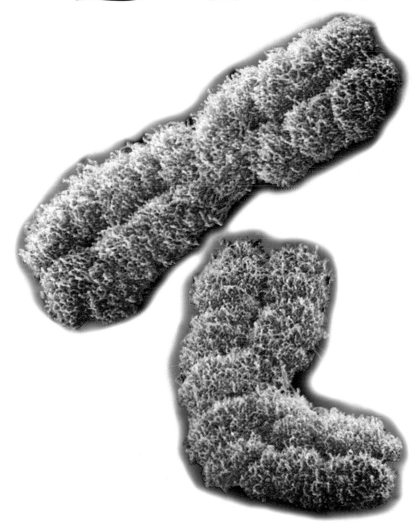

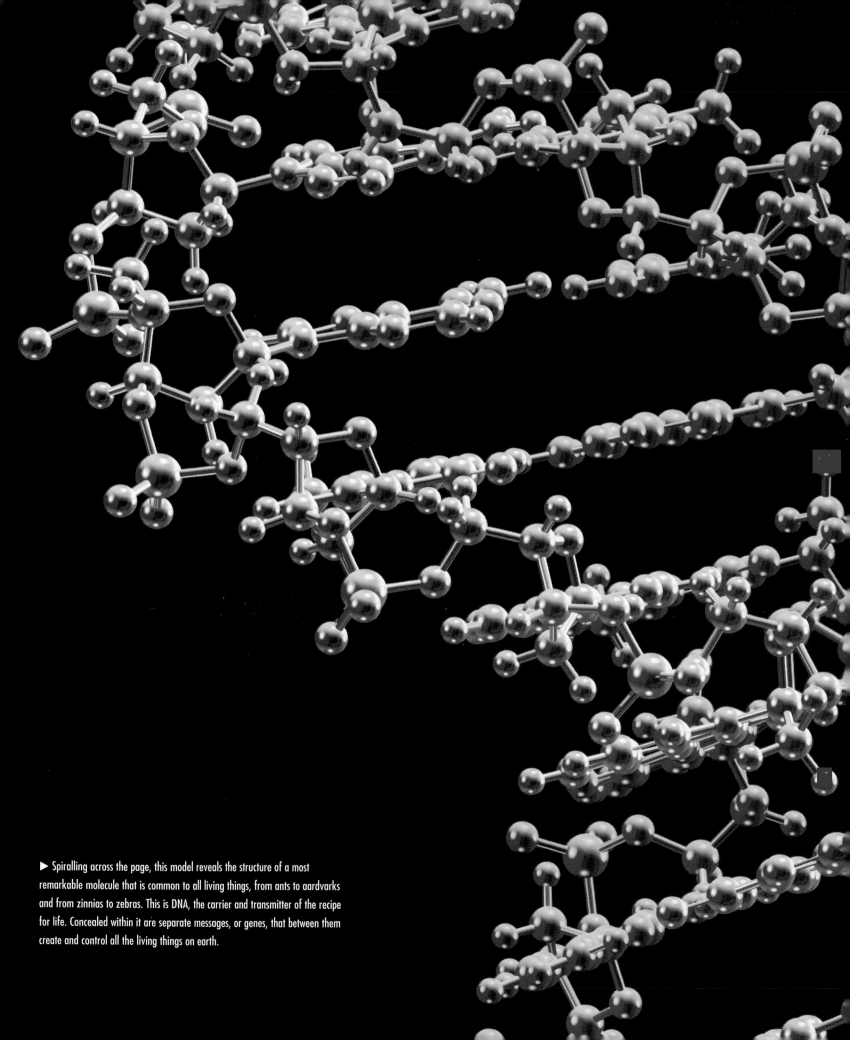

► Spiralling across the page, this model reveals the structure of a most remarkable molecule that is common to all living things, from ants to aardvarks and from zinnias to zebras. This is DNA, the carrier and transmitter of the recipe for life. Concealed within it are separate messages, or genes, that between them create and control all the living things on earth.

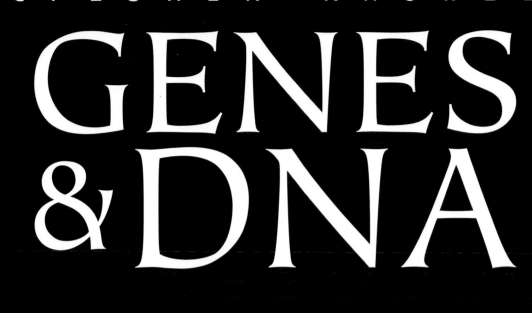

GENES & DNA

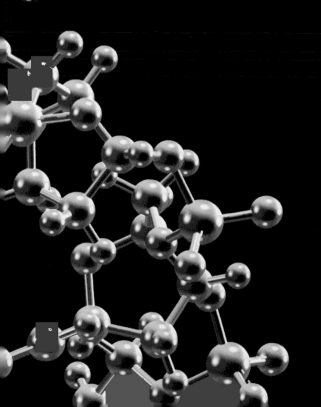

Richard Walker

Foreword by
Steve Jones

KINGFISHER

 KINGFISHER

First published 2003 by Kingfisher

This edition printed 2008 by Kingfisher
an imprint of Macmillan Children's Books
a division of Macmillan Publishers Limited
The Macmillan Building, 4 Crinan Street, London N1 9XW
Basingstoke and Oxford
Associated companies throughout the world
www.panmacmillan.com

Consultant: Professor Alan Teale, University of Stirling

ISBN 978-0-7534-0845-2

Copyright © Macmillan Children's Books 2003

9 8 7 6 5 4 3 2 1
BCA/0408/TWP/MA(MA)/130GRYMA/F

A CIP catalogue record for this book is available from the British Library.

Printed in Singapore

NOTE TO READERS
The website addresses listed in this book are correct at the time of going to print. However, due to the ever-changing nature of the internet, website addresses and content can change. Websites can contain links that are unsuitable for children. The publisher cannot be held responsible for changes in website addresses or content, or for information obtained through third-party websites. We strongly advise that internet searches should be supervised by an adult.

GO FURTHER...
INFORMATION PANEL KEY:

 websites and further reading

 career paths

 places to visit

▼ This electron micrograph captures the process of mitosis in a human kidney. Mitosis is a type of cell division which allows body cells to produce exact copies of themselves. During mitosis, the genetic information in a cell copies itself exactly and identical genes are parcelled into each new daughter cell.

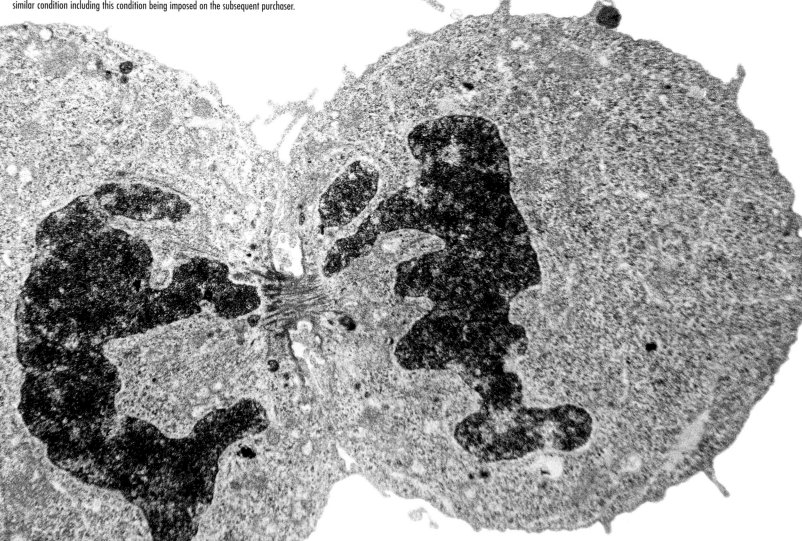

Contents

Foreword

Some of the most important questions in science seem silly, or obvious, but they are not. Why do dogs have puppies and not kittens? Why were you born as a young baby rather than a small but quite elderly adult? And why do you look rather, but not exactly, like your mother and father? Those questions are odd, but they have serious answers. Every one has to do with genetics, the science of inheritance, and for each there is still a great deal we do not understand. However, there is a lot we DO know, and *KFK: Genes & DNA* is the story of what I think is the most exciting part of modern science.

Genetics is amazingly new. When we ask about chemistry – why does iron rust but gold doesn't? – or astronomy – does the Earth go round the Sun or vice versa? – we have to go back hundreds or even thousands of years to track down the great discoveries. Genetics is not like that. Only 150 years ago, everyone, however clever they were, had everything about inheritance wrong. That was odd, because people have always been interested in the subject. Aristocrats are fascinated by pedigrees, farmers have bred from the best animals for thousands of years, and – it seems a fair guess – people have been saying 'Doesn't he look like his Dad?' since long before that.

Once, everyone assumed that children look like their parents because they live in the same way. After all, the children of doctors often become doctors themselves, so why should that not explain why red-haired people have red-haired children? But that does not work. A red-haired woman married to a dark-haired man may have dark- or red-haired children, and sometimes two dark-haired people can have a red-haired child. It was all very baffling.

In 1861, an Austrian monk called Mendel got it right: we do not inherit the hair pigment itself, but sets of instructions – *genes* – from each parent, in a code which is read by the body as it develops. For decades, nobody knew what the code was made of. Then came DNA. Just over 50 years ago, in January 1953, what the molecule of life looked like was quite unknown. In February, Francis Crick and James Watson worked out the structure of DNA, and the double helix was born.

DNA is amazing stuff. When you began, one metre of your father's DNA met one metre of your mother's, to make you – uniquely – into you. Now, just a few years on, the DNA in your own body would stretch to the Moon and back several thousand times. We have read the entire set of instructions that make you what you are. In this book you'll find out how scientists did this, how DNA is copied, how this molecule builds our bodies, how genes tell us where we come from and how genetic engineering may change where we are going.

For a biologist, what is wonderful about genetics is that it is the key to so many apparently different questions. I am (unlike most people) interested in snail genetics (no, I don't eat them), but I have used ideas that came from snails to study fruit flies and even humans. Some of my colleagues work on plants, or on worms, or on frozen mammoths from Siberia – and they all follow the same rules. Turn the page to find out what they are – and just imagine where genetics will get to in 50 years!

Steve Jones.

Professor Steve Jones – geneticist, University College London

CHAPTER 1

Genes and inheritance

This photograph tells a story that we recognize instinctively. Three generations of a family – grandparents, parents and children, including a baby on the way – pose on a beach. We know they are a family because each generation has inherited certain features from the previous one. We know they are all human, but can tell them apart because they each look a little bit different. For thousands of years, how we inherit features, why we look similar but not exactly the same, even how reproduction happens, were all a mystery. Today, as you will discover, science has provided the answer. What we inherit from our parents, and pass on to our children, is an instruction set for life itself – our genes.

Variations on a theme

Imagine standing in a busy street watching people walk by. They all look different, yet all these people are obviously human beings. Why is this? It is because they share a nearly identical set of instructions – with tiny variations between individuals – that builds and runs them, and which they pass on to their children. The same is true of every other living thing on earth.

Building blocks

Living things are made up of tiny cells, that can only be seen under a microscope. Human beings are no exception. Each of us is constructed from around 100 trillion (that is 100,000,000,000,000) of these living building blocks. What's more, these cells contain a copy of a 'master plan'. This set of instructions builds cells and organizes them to form the parts that make up a body. The instructions are called genes, which in turn are made of a remarkable substance called DNA. Scientists are finding out more and more about how genes and DNA work to build our bodies.

Variations on a theme

Is the 'master plan' that constructs a human body identical in all of us? Nearly, but not exactly. For one thing, humans come in two sexes, females and males, who differ in their reproductive systems – the parts that make babies (see pages 18–19). For another, apart from identical twins, all of us vary in terms of height, weight, skin colour, the sound of our voice and a host of other features. Each one of us is a variation on the otherwise constant human theme.

▶ As humans, we all look similar. But because every person has a unique set of features, we can identify each other as friends, family members, famous people or strangers. Some differences between people show wide variations, such as skin colour, which as you can see here varies from very dark to very pale, or hair colour, which varies from black, through brown and red to almost white. Other differences are much more clear-cut.

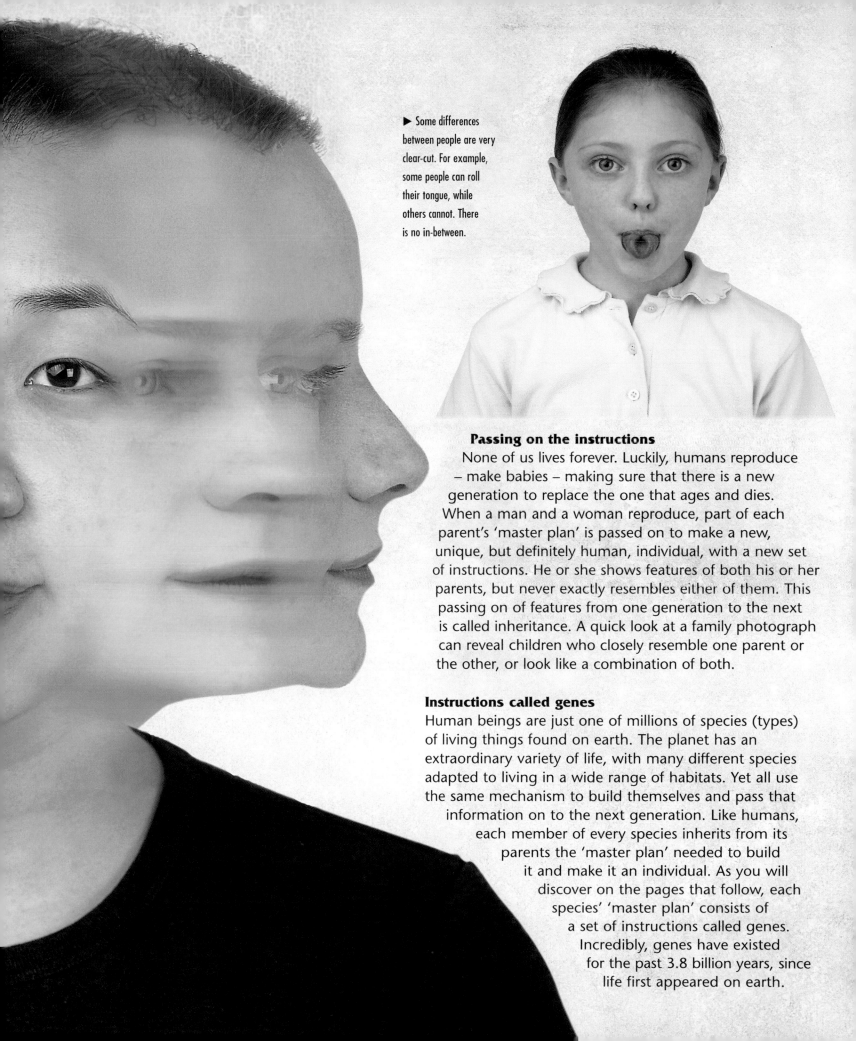

▶ Some differences between people are very clear-cut. For example, some people can roll their tongue, while others cannot. There is no in-between.

Passing on the instructions

None of us lives forever. Luckily, humans reproduce – make babies – making sure that there is a new generation to replace the one that ages and dies. When a man and a woman reproduce, part of each parent's 'master plan' is passed on to make a new, unique, but definitely human, individual, with a new set of instructions. He or she shows features of both his or her parents, but never exactly resembles either of them. This passing on of features from one generation to the next is called inheritance. A quick look at a family photograph can reveal children who closely resemble one parent or the other, or look like a combination of both.

Instructions called genes

Human beings are just one of millions of species (types) of living things found on earth. The planet has an extraordinary variety of life, with many different species adapted to living in a wide range of habitats. Yet all use the same mechanism to build themselves and pass that information on to the next generation. Like humans, each member of every species inherits from its parents the 'master plan' needed to build it and make it an individual. As you will discover on the pages that follow, each species' 'master plan' consists of a set of instructions called genes. Incredibly, genes have existed for the past 3.8 billion years, since life first appeared on earth.

Discovering genes

From the earliest times, people have realized that parents pass on features to their offspring. Human children are like their parents, sheep and cattle are like their parents and wheat plants are like their parent plants. People also believed that parents' features blended together in the offspring, like paints being mixed on a palette. But no-one knew how inheritance really worked until the answer was provided by a monk called Gregor Mendel.

Selective breeding

For centuries, farmers have bred from animals and plants with useful characteristics, for example sheep with thicker fleeces and bigger bodies, or crop plants with more seeds. They have done this in the hope that the offspring would inherit these features. But until the mid-19th century, how inheritance worked was a mystery. Did features blend together? Why did some features disappear in one generation only to reappear in the next?

Monk and scientist

In 1843, an Austrian monk, Gregor Mendel entered the monastery of Brünn in Austria (now Brno in the Czech Republic). As well as being a monk, he studied science and was a keen gardener. From 1856, he started to use the monastery garden as a laboratory.

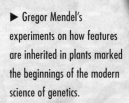

▶ Gregor Mendel's experiments on how features are inherited in plants marked the beginnings of the modern science of genetics.

Looking at peas

Mendel chose the garden pea plant for his experiments. Pea plants show certain clear-cut features that are easily identified. For example, they can be either tall or short (never medium-sized), and have either purple or white flowers. Mendel wanted to find out how these characteristics are passed on. To understand Mendel's experiments, it is helpful to know how pea plants reproduce. Male and female sex organs are found together inside a pea flower. Tiny male pollen grains are carried to the female organs in a process called pollination. A seed is formed, and this grows into a new pea plant.

Crossing experiments ·

One of the features Mendel studied was flower colour. He took plants with purple flowers and plants with white flowers and 'crossed' these. He carefully used a paintbrush to transfer pollen from a purple flower to a white one, and vice versa. He planted the resulting seeds and noted the flower colour of the offspring plants. Then he allowed the offspring to pollinate and produce seeds. He planted these seeds and again observed the results.

◀ This 18th-century painting shows a sheep produced by selective breeding. The farmer who bred it knew that by mating a ram and a ewe with the 'right' features, such as a thick fleece, he would hopefully get offspring with the same characteristics.

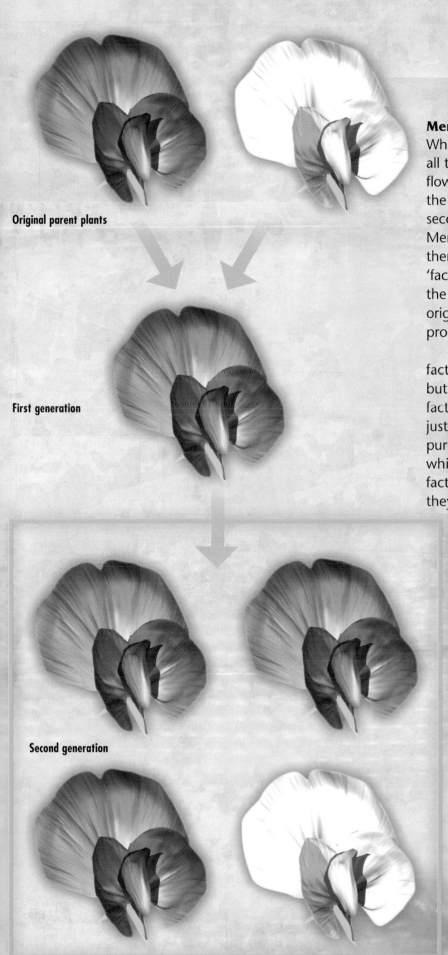

Original parent plants

First generation

Second generation

◄ Mendel crossed purple- and white-flowered plants. All the offspring in the first generation had purple flowers. But the white flowers had not disappeared. When the first generation plants produced offspring, about one in four of these second generation plants turned out to have white flowers.

Mendel's 'factors'

When the purple- and white-flowered plants were crossed, all the offspring – called the first generation – had purple flowers. But the white features had not disappeared. When the new plants produced offspring of their own – the second generation – some of these had white flowers. Mendel brilliantly suggested that inside each pea plant there were tiny units of inheritance, which he called 'factors'. He did not know what these were or where in the plant they were found, but he worked out that each original parent plant carried pairs of identical factors that produced either purple or white flowers.

In the first generation, each plant inherited a purple factor from one parent and a white factor from the other, but was purple-flowered. Mendel explained that the purple factors were dominant to the white factors. In other words, just one purple factor was enough to make the flowers purple. In the second generation, some of the plants were white-flowered because they had inherited only white factors. Mendel called the white factors recessive because they had receded, or disappeared, in the first generation.

The birth of genetics

With his theory of factors, Mendel showed that characteristics are not blended like paints on a palette when they are passed on to new generations, but remain separate. His pioneering work was still unrecognized when he died in 1884, but it was rediscovered in the early 20th century by scientists researching inheritance. Mendel's factors were given a new name. They were called genes. His work became the basis of the science of genetics.

► Pea plants grow and reproduce rapidly and produce lots of offspring in a year. This made them a good choice of plant for Mendel's experiments, as it meant he got plenty of results in a short time.

Gene carriers

Scientists in the 1880s devised new ways of examining cells under the microscope. For the first time, they saw long, thread-like structures inside the cells, which they named chromosomes. By the early 1900s, they worked out that these chromosomes carry the factors, or genes, that control the features we inherit from our parents. They also contain the instructions a cell needs to function.

Cells and chromosomes

As the basic units of life, cells may be tiny but that does not mean they are simple. Cells consist of many different components that co-operate to make the cell work. At the core of operations is the cell's control centre – the nucleus. The cell membrane is a flexible barrier, sausage-shaped mitochondria provide the cell's energy needs, and a structure called endoplasmic reticulum is like a tiny factory, making essential substances.

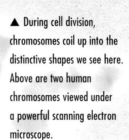

▲ During cell division, chromosomes coil up into the distinctive shapes we see here. Above are two human chromosomes viewed under a powerful scanning electron microscope.

▼ This is a human karyotype, a full set of chromosomes – 46 (23 pairs) in total. Here the chromosomes are arranged in size order from largest (1) to smallest (22). The 23rd pair is the sex chromosomes (see pages 18–19) – here female (XX).

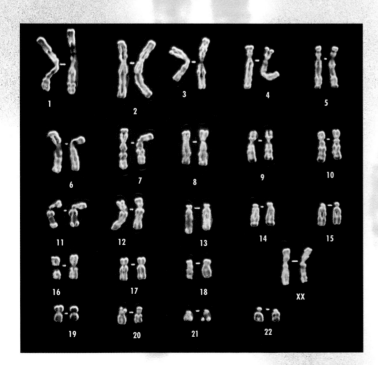

Chromosomes and genes

Packed inside the nucleus are chromosomes. For most of the time, these take the form of long, very thin threads, which are hard to see. But when a cell divides to make new cells, the long threads coil up and shorten to form chromosomes like these, visible under a powerful microscope. These are where the instruction kits of genes are to be found. Experiments have shown that, rather than being scattered everywhere, the thousands of genes occur in strict sequence along our chromosomes.

Two sets of chromosomes

In 1903, American scientist Walter Sutton discovered that most cells are diploid – from the Greek for 'double' – which means they contain two sets of chromosomes. In the two sets, chromosomes occur in matching pairs, and matching chromosomes carry the same genes at the same positions along their length.

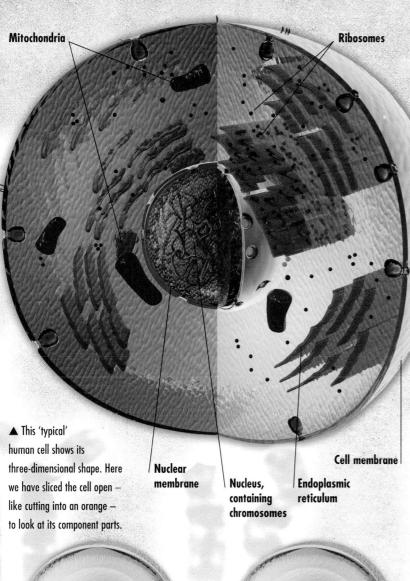

Mitochondria

Ribosomes

▲ This 'typical' human cell shows its three-dimensional shape. Here we have sliced the cell open — like cutting into an orange — to look at its component parts.

Nuclear membrane

Nucleus, containing chromosomes

Endoplasmic reticulum

Cell membrane

How many chromosomes?

If humans have 46 chromosomes, what about other living things? Scientists have shown that each species of organism has its own precise chromosome number, unrelated to how big or complex it might be. Cells from an 84m tall giant redwood tree have 22 chromosomes, while cells from the much smaller goldfish have 94. Our closest relatives – chimpanzees and gorillas – have 48 chromosomes, as does the potato! What really matters, in terms of what an organism looks like or how it works, is what genes are carried by those chromosomes.

Dividing cells

Each cell contains all the instructions it needs to function, but cells do not last for ever. Our bodies continue to grow through childhood and then, as adults, to replace worn-out cells. Growth and repair are both possible because cells divide. During cell division, each cell splits to produce two identical 'daughter' cells. Key to this process is mitosis, or nuclear division. Mitosis divides a cell's nucleus exactly, parcelling out identical packs of gene-carrying chromosomes to each new cell. Each new cell has exactly the same genes as the old one.

1. Chromosomes start to shorten and thicken

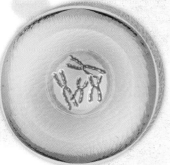

2. Chromosomes form X shapes

3. Chromosomes line up

◀ Before mitosis starts, the thread-like chromosomes get shorter and thicker (1). Each chromosome also copies itself, producing two linked identical 'arms' – called chromatids – that give it a distinctive X shape (2). The nuclear membrane disintegrates and the chromosomes line up across the centre of the cell (3). Then the chromatids are pulled apart towards each end of the cell (4). Two new nuclear membranes form and the cell begins to split in two (5). Finally, two identical new 'daughter' cells result (6).

4. Chromatids are pulled apart

5. New nuclear membranes form

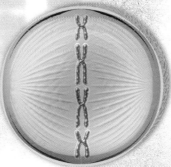

6. Two identical new cells form

New generations

Each of us is a new invention, similar to, but never quite the same as, anyone else. This is because every one of us has a unique set of genes. Half of these genes were passed on from our mother, and half from our father. When our parents reproduced, they contributed equally to a novel package of genes that contained all the instructions to make a brand new person.

Special division

A new individual is made from cells called sex cells – sperm and eggs. Sperm are formed in the testes of men, and eggs are formed in the ovaries of women (see pages 18–19), by a special type of cell division called meiosis. Sex cells are special because they have only 23 chromosomes – half the usual number. The cells that produce sex cells have two sets of 23 chromosomes (46 in total), like other body cells. During meiosis, these cells split so that each resulting sperm or egg contains just one set of 23 chromosomes, a unique mix of the original two sets. In addition, many chromosomes swap genes with each other during a process called crossing over. This further shuffles the original combination of genes to make brand new combinations in the resulting sperm or egg cells.

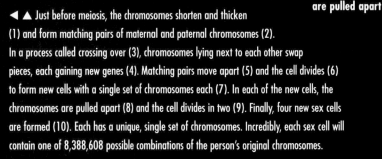

4. New combinations result

5. Matching pairs move apart

6. Cell starts to divide

7. New cells are formed

3. Crossing over takes place

8. Chromosomes are pulled apart

9. The cells divide in two

2. Matching pairs form

1. Chromosomes shorten and thicken

◄ ▲ Just before meiosis, the chromosomes shorten and thicken (1) and form matching pairs of maternal and paternal chromosomes (2). In a process called crossing over (3), chromosomes lying next to each other swap pieces, each gaining new genes (4). Matching pairs move apart (5) and the cell divides (6) to form new cells with a single set of chromosomes each (7). In each of the new cells, the chromosomes are pulled apart (8) and the cell divides in two (9). Finally, four new sex cells are formed (10). Each has a unique, single set of chromosomes. Incredibly, each sex cell will contain one of 8,388,608 possible combinations of the person's original chromosomes.

10. Four new sex cells result

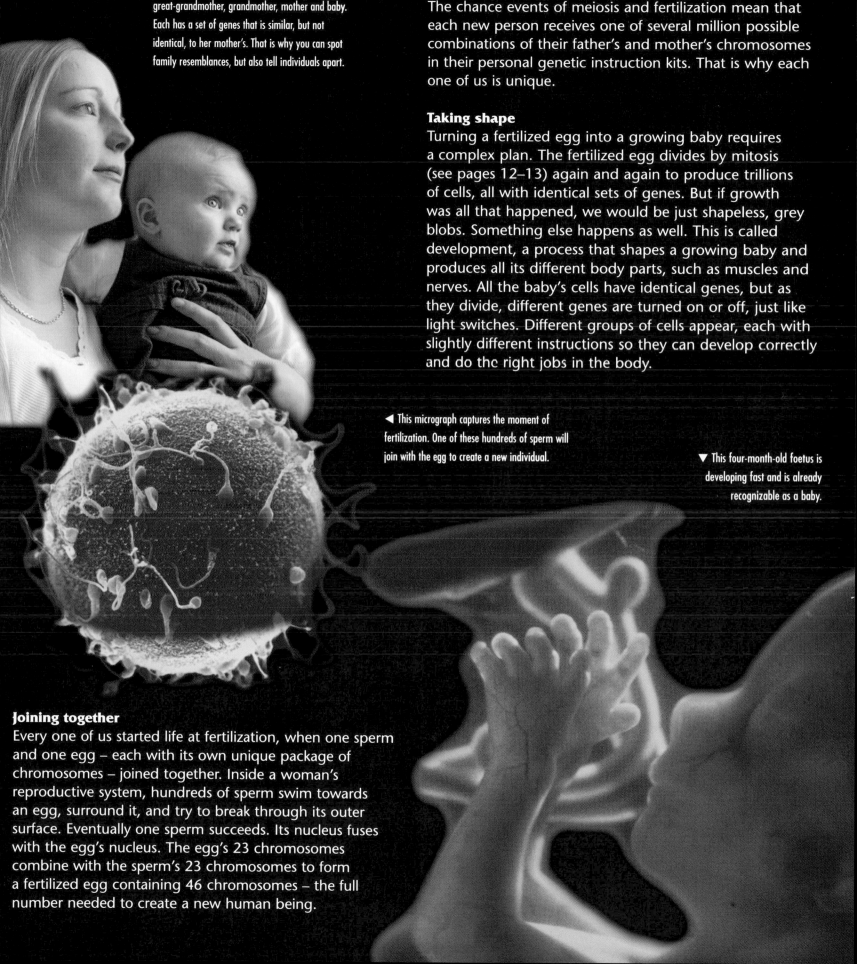

great-grandmother, grandmother, mother and baby. Each has a set of genes that is similar, but not identical, to her mother's. That is why you can spot family resemblances, but also tell individuals apart.

The chance events of meiosis and fertilization mean that each new person receives one of several million possible combinations of their father's and mother's chromosomes in their personal genetic instruction kits. That is why each one of us is unique.

Taking shape

Turning a fertilized egg into a growing baby requires a complex plan. The fertilized egg divides by mitosis (see pages 12–13) again and again to produce trillions of cells, all with identical sets of genes. But if growth was all that happened, we would be just shapeless, grey blobs. Something else happens as well. This is called development, a process that shapes a growing baby and produces all its different body parts, such as muscles and nerves. All the baby's cells have identical genes, but as they divide, different genes are turned on or off, just like light switches. Different groups of cells appear, each with slightly different instructions so they can develop correctly and do the right jobs in the body.

◄ This micrograph captures the moment of fertilization. One of these hundreds of sperm will join with the egg to create a new individual.

▼ This four-month-old foetus is developing fast and is already recognizable as a baby.

Joining together

Every one of us started life at fertilization, when one sperm and one egg – each with its own unique package of chromosomes – joined together. Inside a woman's reproductive system, hundreds of sperm swim towards an egg, surround it, and try to break through its outer surface. Eventually one sperm succeeds. Its nucleus fuses with the egg's nucleus. The egg's 23 chromosomes combine with the sperm's 23 chromosomes to form a fertilized egg containing 46 chromosomes – the full number needed to create a new human being.

Gene variation

Genes are the instructions needed to construct a human body and all its features. Compare one person to another and you will find that their genes are very similar. But there are some differences, or variations. Without them, we would all be identical. We inherit these variations from our parents, and may pass them on to our children.

Like beads on a string

Inside human cells, as we have already seen, there are 23 pairs of chromosomes. One in each pair is maternal (from the mother) and the other is paternal (from the father). Each set of chromosomes carries between 30,000 and 40,000 genes, arranged along the chromosomes like beads on a string. Genes occur in exactly the same order along the lengths of both the chromosomes in a pair. So genes, as well as chromosomes, occur in pairs.

Variation through alleles

Each chromosome in a matching pair of maternal and paternal chromosomes is nearly, but not quite, a mirror image of the other. Like different flavours of ice cream, a gene that controls a particular feature can come in two or more versions known as alleles. It is alleles that produce the variations – such as brown eyes or blue eyes – that make us all a bit different.

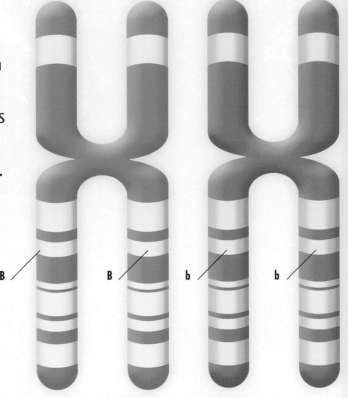

▲ The gene controlling the colour of your eyes is found at the same position, or locus, on both maternal and paternal versions of chromosome 15. It has two alleles. One, labelled B, produces brown eyes, and the other, labelled b, produces blue eyes. A pair of chromosomes could have BB, Bb or bb alleles.

▼ This brother and sister are closely related but the boy has blue eyes, and the girl brown, because they have not inherited exactly the same alleles for eye colour from their parents.

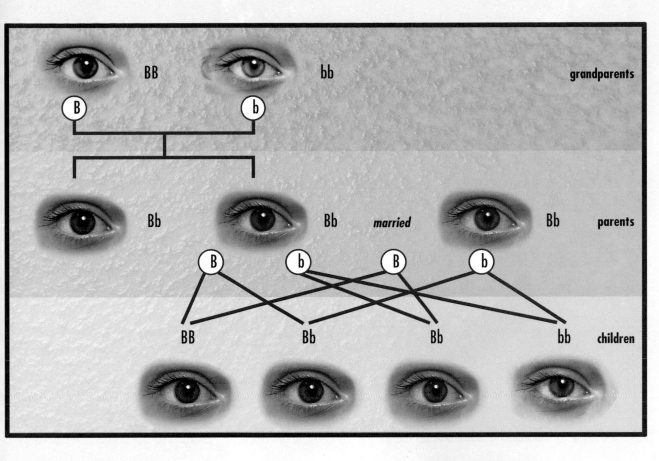

Dominant and recessive

Using eye colour alleles as an example, we can look at how alleles are passed on from parents to children, and find out why sometimes alleles do not actually produce a particular feature even when they are present. Alleles are usually given letters – the allele for brown eyes is usually labelled with a capital B, and the allele for blue eyes is usually labelled with a lower case b. A person who has both types of allele – B and b – will have brown eyes. Why? Because the brown allele, referred to as dominant, has an effect. It masks or overrides the blue allele, which is less powerful and is called the recessive allele. A person with two brown alleles (BB) will have brown eyes. Only a person with two blue alleles (bb) will have blue eyes.

Altered genes

How do alleles, these different versions of genes, actually appear? Through random changes called mutations (see pages 32–33). These can happen naturally, or they may be caused by someone being exposed to radiation or harmful chemicals. Whatever the cause, everyone has several mutations among the genes on their chromosomes. A mutation may produce an allele that has no noticeable effect, one that produces a useful change or one that causes harm. If it occurs in a cell that produces egg or sperm it may be passed on to the next generation.

Understanding alleles

Now we know more about chromosomes, genes and alleles, we can see why Gregor Mendel (see pages 10–11) got the results he did when he carried out his experiments with pea plants. What Mendel identified as 'factors' we now know are genes or alleles. We can work out that Mendel's original purple- and white-flowered plants had pairs of identical alleles. The allele producing purple flowers was dominant to that producing white. Only the plants with two white alleles had white flowers.

▼ Fruit flies are commonly used in research to help us understand genes and alleles. On the left is a normal fruit fly and on the right is one treated with radiation. The treated fruit fly has gene mutations that cause its red eyes to be smaller.

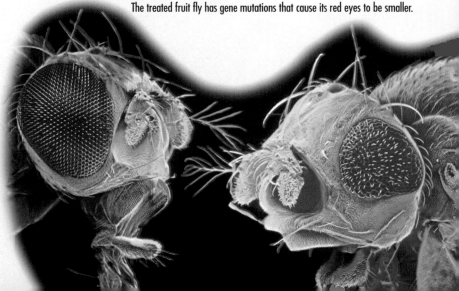

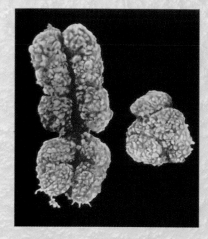

▲ This photograph of the sex chromosomes of a human male – X on the left and Y on the right – clearly shows how much smaller the male Y chromosome is. It has far fewer genes.

Girl or boy?

We become aware at an early age that people are divided into two distinct groups, or sexes, called females and males. Why is this so important? Because it takes two parents, one of each sex, to reproduce and make babies. Whether a baby turns out to be female or male – a girl or a boy – depends on one particular chromosome inherited from its father, which makes up part of a pair of chromosomes called the sex chromosomes. Girls have two X chromosomes, while boys have an X and a Y.

▼ Just one chromosome inherited from their father determines these children's sex. The girl inherited her father's X chromosome and the boy inherited his Y chromosome.

Two sexes

Boys and girls are different in some ways and similar in others. In terms of biology, the main difference is in their reproductive systems – the parts of the body that, when they become adults, will allow them to have babies of their own. When humans reproduce, two individuals – a male and a female – are needed. Males have two testes that in adult men make sex cells called sperm. Females have two ovaries that in adult women release sex cells called eggs. If sperm and egg meet at fertilization (see pages 14–15), a new baby, with its unique combination of genes, starts to grow inside the woman's uterus. As we have already learned, reproduction results in offspring which are not identical to their parents. We inherit some of our parents' features but not others.

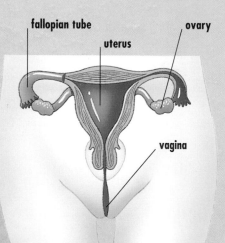

fallopian tube   ovary

uterus

vagina

▲ Females have two ovaries. These are where meiosis occurs and egg cells are made. Eggs are released from the ovaries into the fallopian tubes. If sperm and egg meet, a fertilized egg embeds itself in the lining of the uterus, where it starts to grow into a new baby.

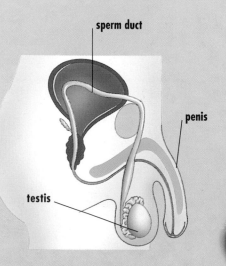

sperm duct

penis

testis

▲ Males have two testes. Here, meiosis occurs and millions of sperm cells are made. When a man and a woman reproduce, sperm travel along the sperm duct and out through the penis. If a sperm meets an egg cell, fertilization occurs.

XX or XY?

A person's sex depends on just two of the 46 chromosomes inside his or her cells – the sex chromosomes. A girl has two X chromosomes (XX). A boy has one X and one Y chromosome (XY). Eggs and sperm are the exception to this rule. Since they have only 23 chromosomes, they have only one of the pair of sex chromosomes. All eggs carry an X chromosome. Half of all sperm carry an X chromosome and half carry a Y.

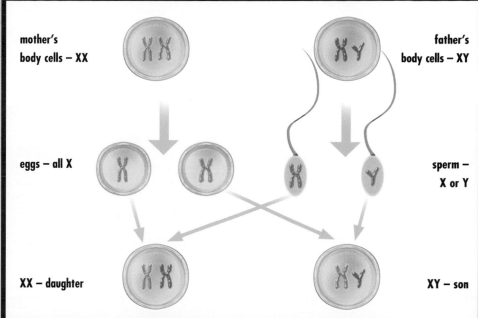

mother's body cells – XX

father's body cells – XY

eggs – all X

sperm – X or Y

XX – daughter

XY – son

▲ Meiosis produces sex cells that have only half the number of chromosomes found in a normal body cell. Each sex cell has a single sex chromosome – X or Y. Fertilization joins egg cells (all X) with sperm cells (X or Y). The possible combinations that result are XX – female – or XY – male.

Male switch

Why does being XX make someone a girl, and being XY a boy? In early weeks of pregnancy, about five weeks after fertilization, something happens inside XY embryos. A gene, called *SRY*, which is carried by the Y chromosome, is switched on. It sends out a message that triggers the growth of testes and other male parts, so the embryo develops into a baby boy. An embryo with two X chromosomes does not have the *SRY* gene, and becomes a baby girl.

Inheritance linked to sex

Some conditions, such as colour blindness, are much more common in boys than girls. This is because the recessive allele that causes colour blindness is carried on the X chromosome, but not on the Y. If the allele is present on a male's single X chromosome there is no dominant allele in the equivalent position on the Y chromosome to override the recessive allele. So the male will be colour blind. In a female, both X chromosomes would have to carry the recessive colour blindness allele to make her colour blind. That is why so few girls are colour blind.

► Some people who are colour blind cannot see the difference between red and green. If you can see the green line of dots in this pattern, you are not colour blind.

Nature or nurture?

The genes you inherited from your parents determine what you look like and influence how you behave. Or do they? What about your environment – all the influences in your life before and since you were born? Don't they have an effect as well? People have argued for years about whether it is your genes (nature) or your environment (nurture) that make you who you are. Today, scientists are finding out more about the way nature and nurture interact.

▲ The boy on the right has albinism, a condition produced wholly by genes. Unlike the boy on the left, his skin lacks the brown pigment melanin, which gives skin its colour. He has a version of the melanin-producing gene that stops melanin from being made.

Moulding the framework

Genes provide the plan for our bodies. But this plan can be moulded and changed in lots of ways by our surroundings and behaviour. One important influence is the conditions inside our mother's uterus, where we spend our first nine months. Others include the food we eat, where we live, the education we receive, even how active we are, as well as the influence of family and friends.

Just genes

There are some features that are controlled by genes alone. Eye colour is one example (see pages 16–17). Another is a person's blood group. Everyone belongs to one of four blood groups, called A, B, AB, and O. Which one you belong to – and you may already know this – is determined by a gene. So, regardless of the way you are brought up, your blood group cannot change.

▶ A baby inherits his or her genes from his or her parents, and they look after or nurture him or her. But a person's environment – where and how he or she lives – is also a part of that nurturing and crucial to the way he or she will turn out. Diet, education, healthcare, wealth and way of life will all play a part. These things vary greatly from country to country.

Nurturing change

In most cases it is not genes alone but genes and environment that contribute towards making us who we are. Take height, for example. The average height in western countries has increased dramatically in the last 400 years. That is because, although genes play a part in determining how tall we are (as you will know if there are lots of tall people in your family), better food and living conditions have caused us to grow taller. A child who grows up without plentiful food and a safe environment may be much smaller than average. However, it is important to remember that whatever we obtain from our surroundings will not be passed on to our offspring, because it is not part of our genes. Sumo wrestlers, for example, will not necessarily father overweight children.

▲ It is not just genes that make these sumo wrestlers so big. Diet plays an important part — they deliberately pile on extra weight by eating large amounts of a special rich stew called chanko.

Personality and genes?

As humans, 99.9 per cent of our genes are exactly the same as those of everyone else. Yet that 0.1 per cent difference is enough, combined with the effects of our surroundings, to make us the individuals we are. Look at your friends and family and you will see how much personalities differ. Studying personality, as well as intelligence, creativity and so on, is so complex that scientists are only just starting to understand how nature or nurture shapes each aspect of who we are. For example, a gene has been discovered that plays a part in making some people thrill-seekers, enjoying activities such as dangerous sports. But it is only one of many genes — not to mention the effects of environment — that may make us daredevils or stay-at-homes.

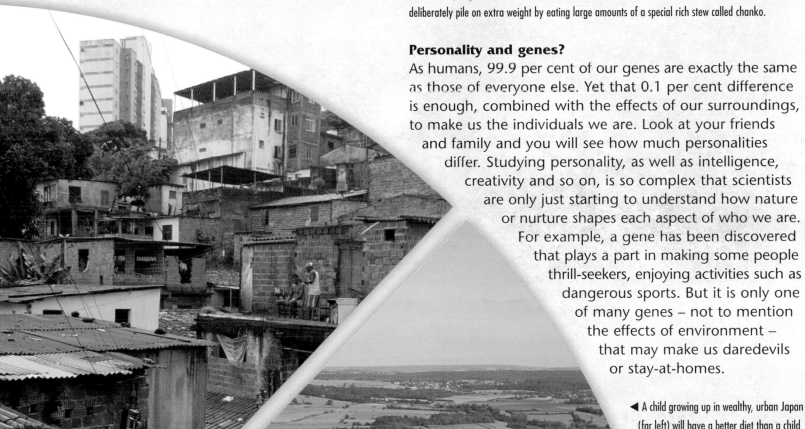

◀ A child growing up in wealthy, urban Japan (far left) will have a better diet than a child in a village in Papua New Guinea (centre left), and is likely to live much longer, to an average age of 82 rather than just 65. In Brazil, where many people live in slums such as those in San Salvador, (centre right), six per cent of children are underweight. In Europe (right), a diet rich in fatty foods can lead to obesity and heart disease in later life.

Two of a kind

Animals vary in the number of offspring they have. Cats, for example, can have up to eight kittens. Humans, on the other hand, usually have just one baby at a time, but occasionally give birth to two babies, called twins. Twins can help us understand more about genes and inheritance. Scientists study whether certain features are inherited or whether they are caused by a person's surroundings.

▲ Identical twins often look so similar that they manage to confuse everyone. They have identical sets of chromosomes and genes. Identical twins are always either both females or both males because they have identical sex chromosomes.

The same or different

As you probably know, twins come in two varieties – identical and non-identical (or fraternal). Identical twins look exactly – or very, very nearly – the same. This is because they both have exactly the same genes. Non-identical twins are the same age and grow in their mother's uterus at the same time, but otherwise they are no more alike than any other brothers and sisters would be. Each has his or her unique combination of genes.

▼ Identical twins usually grow up in the same surroundings, and often develop similar interests. However, a particular musical ability, called perfect pitch, is shown by twin studies to be largely genetic.

Studying twins

Twins have been studied for years by scientists investigating whether human characteristics are the result of nature (genes) or nurture (environment), or both. Because identical twins share the same genes, if a feature is shared by most pairs of identical twins but not by most non-identical twins, scientists deduce that it is more likely to be determined by genes. But if it is a feature that is shared by similar numbers of pairs of identical and non-identical twins, it is more likely to be influenced by surroundings. Most features, however, result from a mix of genes and environment.

How twins happen

To see how twins happen we need to look at what goes on during fertilization. Normally, a woman releases one egg from one of her ovaries once a month. If the egg is fertilized by a sperm, it will start to grow into a baby. But, as shown in the diagram above right, sometimes events go slightly differently, resulting in twins.

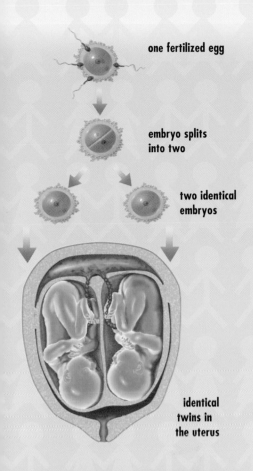

one fertilized egg

embryo splits into two

two identical embryos

identical twins in the uterus

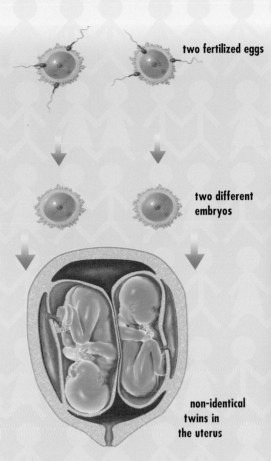

two fertilized eggs

two different embryos

non-identical twins in the uterus

▲ Identical twins happen when one egg is fertilized but then at some stage before reaching the uterus it splits into two completely separate but identical embryos. Inside the uterus, identical twins each have their own umbilical cord but share the same placenta.

▲ Non-identical twins happen when two eggs are released from the ovaries and fertilized by two different sperm. Inside the uterus, the arrangement of non-identical twins is usually different from that of identical twins.

▲ Non-identical twins can look very similar or very different, just like other sets of brothers and sisters. They do not share exactly the same chromosomes and genes but have different combinations of their parents' genes. They can be sisters, brothers or (as here) a brother and sister.

More than two

Humans very rarely have more than one or two babies at a time. But it does sometimes happen. Even rarer than having twins is giving birth to three babies, or triplets. On average, one birth in 70 produces twins, and just one birth in every 2,000 results in triplets. Usually triplets are non-identical, but they can be identical or even consist of two identical triplets and one non-identical brother or sister. In a very few pregnancies, four (quadruplets), five (quintuplets) or even six babies (sextuplets) may be born. This usually happens when the mother is having fertility treatment to help her become pregnant.

▶ Janet and Graham Walton's daughters Kate, Lucy, Jenny and Ruth (back row), and Hannah and Sarah (front row) are a set of all-girl sextuplets. They made headlines when they were born in Liverpool, England, in 1983.

SUMMARY OF CHAPTER 1: GENES AND INHERITANCE

Inheriting features

How do humans, and other living things, inherit features from their parents? How are those features passed on to their offspring? Why do we all look a bit different? These are the questions raised in Chapter 1, and we have seen that it is possible to answer them using genetics, a science founded on the research of a 19th-century monk, Gregor Mendel.

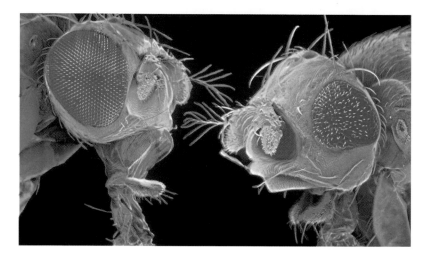

Genes are instructions

In Mendel's time, people believed that when a man and woman reproduced, their features blended together in their child. Mendel carried out experiments on plants which showed that what parents actually pass on to their offspring are tiny units of inheritance that do not blend, but remain separate. He called these units 'factors'. We now call them genes. Each gene is an instruction that controls a particular feature, such as eye colour. Genes are found inside cells on long, thread-like structures called chromosomes, of which there are two sets. Genes come in pairs, and genes in a pair can occur in different forms, called alleles, that produce different versions of the same feature, such as blue or brown eyes. That explains why we all vary a bit.

Nature and nurture

Not every aspect of our lives depends on our genes. Our genes (nature) provide a framework that is moulded by all the experiences we have in life (nurture). We can test the influences of nature and nurture by comparing similarities between identical twins, who share exactly the same genes.

Go further...

To discover lots more about genes and DNA, visit: www.dnaftb.org

Sort chromosomes into pairs and play other gene games at:
www.genecrc.org/site/ko/ko5.htm

See an animation of mitosis at:
www.cellsalive.com/mitosis.htm
or of meiosis at:
www.rothamsted.bbsrc.ac.uk/notebook
/courses/guide/movie/meiosis.htm

Learn more about nature and nurture, twins, and lots more besides at:
www.bbc.co.uk/science/genes

The Language of the Genes by Steve Jones (HarperCollins, 1993) – for older readers

Botanist
Studies plants and the way they live and reproduce.

Cytologist
Studies cells, their structure, and the way they work.

Geneticist
Studies genes, DNA and inheritance.

Microscopist
Examines and photographs small objects, such as chromosomes, using a light or electron microscope.

Psychologist
Studies the mind and human behaviour.

Visit the Mendel Museum of Genetics at the abbey where Mendel carried out his experiments:
www.mendel-museum.org
Abbey of St Thomas,
Brno,
Czech Republic
T: +420 (0)5 43 42 40 43

Take a fascinating tour of what makes you you in the Who am I? gallery at the Science Museum:
www.sciencemuseum.org.uk
Exhibition Road,
London SW7
T: 0870 870 4771

CHAPTER 2

DNA: the molecule of life

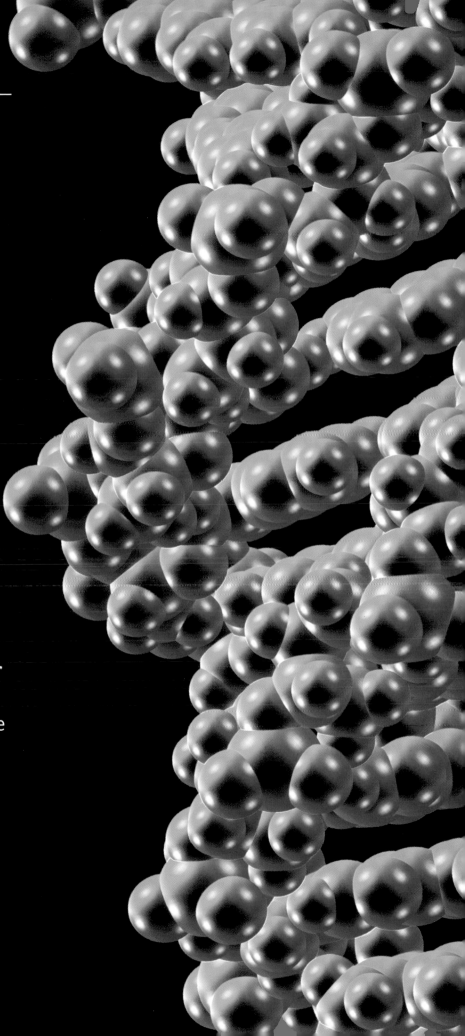

A time span of 50 years is insignificant compared to the billions of years that life has existed on earth. But the 50 years between 1953 and 2003 are of huge significance to biology because it was during that half century that many of the secrets of life were revealed. The trigger for these revelations was one of the great science feats of all time – the discovery of the structure of DNA, the material from which genes are made. Once DNA's structure was known, scientists were able to work out how it provides a library of instructions which control the cells that make up our bodies, and those of all other living things. At the beginning of the 21st century, the Human Genome Project made another great leap forward by completing the enormous task of reading the letters that make up the instructions contained in our DNA. This achievement marks the start of a process that one day will allow humans to understand completely how DNA makes us all human beings, but also makes us unique individuals.

Discovering DNA

For nearly four billion years, DNA – or deoxyribonucleic acid – has been the carrier of genetic information inside earth's living things. DNA is the key to life. Our own knowledge of this vital molecule is much more recent. Only in 1953 did scientists uncover the secrets of DNA's structure. But the DNA story begins some 80 years earlier than this.

Looking inside the nucleus

In 1869, a Swiss doctor called Johann Friedrich Miescher was studying white blood cells extracted from pus-soaked bandages. He managed to isolate the nuclei of these cells (nuclei is the plural of nucleus). When he analyzed the chemicals inside the nuclei he discovered a new substance that he called nuclein. This chemical was later named deoxyribonucleic acid, or DNA for short.

Scientists already knew that genes are found inside the nucleus. So does this mean they are made of DNA? Despite Miescher's findings, few scientists thought this was true. Most felt that genetic material might be found not in DNA but in substances called proteins (see pages 30–31). It was not until 1944 that Canadian-born scientist Oswald Avery finally proved that DNA – not proteins – carried the cell's genetic instructions.

▲ Important evidence about DNA's structure came from X-ray diffraction photographs like this one. The pattern suggests that DNA is made up of two long chains that spiral around each other. This spiral shape is called a double helix.

◄ Rosalind Franklin played an important role in the discovery of DNA. Her X-ray diffraction photographs provided vital clues about the shape of the DNA molecule, which Watson and Crick built on to make their momentous discovery.

Building models

Meanwhile in Cambridge, England, American biologist James Watson and British physicist Francis Crick were also determined to find out DNA's secrets. In 1952, they started building three-dimensional models, trying to fit together in the right proportions the components they knew to be the building blocks of DNA. They struggled to find the right combination until, in January 1953, they had a stroke of luck.

Success at last

Rosalind Franklin's senior colleague, Maurice Wilkins, showed Watson and Crick – without her knowledge – Franklin's X-ray diffraction photograph of DNA. They recognized immediately that this was the missing part of the jigsaw that would help them work out the structure of the DNA molecule. On 28th February 1953, Watson and Crick successfully completed their model of DNA. Their confidence in being right was summed up by Crick when he said to friends, "We've discovered the secret of life". Watson, Crick and Wilkins shared the 1962 Nobel Prize for medicine, for the greatest biological discovery of the 20th century. Sadly, Franklin did not share the honour. She had died four years earlier in 1958.

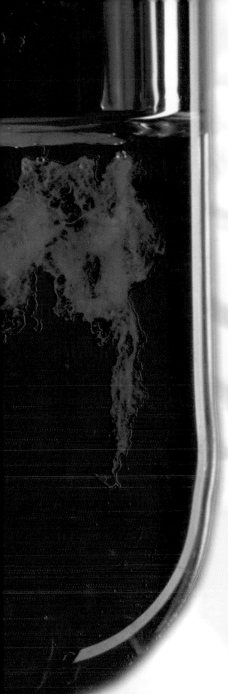

◀ DNA is an extremely long molecule. Here it is visible as long, stringy threads.

▶ James Watson (right) and Francis Crick (far right) pose with their model of the DNA molecule. They published their revolutionary findings on 25th April 1953.

On the trail

The race was on to discover how DNA worked. To do that, scientists needed to understand its structure. British scientist Rosalind Franklin, working at King's College, London, made great advances towards this goal by using a technique called X-ray crystallography. Franklin passed X-rays – like the ones used to 'see' bones inside the body – through DNA crystals. These X-rays were bent, or diffracted, as they bounced off the atoms inside the DNA molecule. When they emerged, the pattern of bent X-rays, caught on film as a photograph called an X-ray diffraction pattern, revealed that the components of the DNA molecule fit together in a spiral or helix shape.

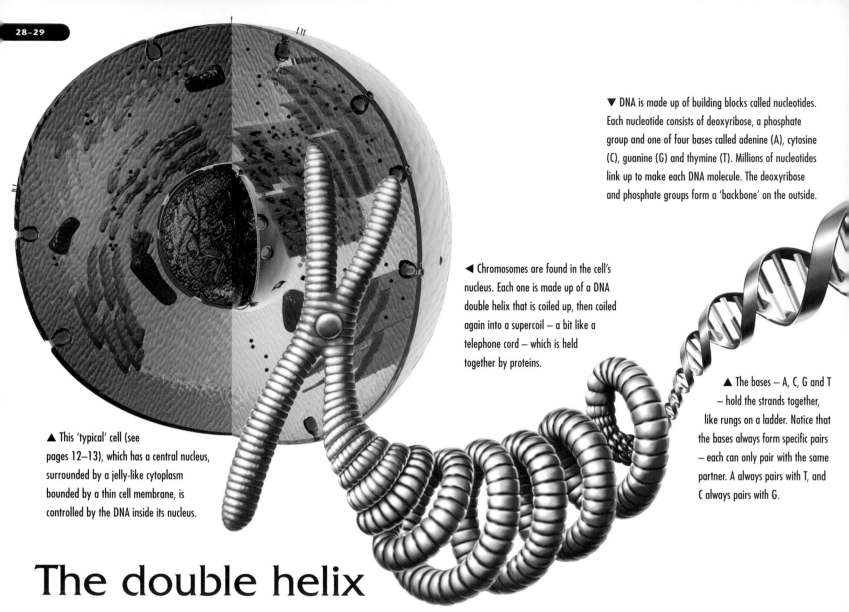

▼ DNA is made up of building blocks called nucleotides. Each nucleotide consists of deoxyribose, a phosphate group and one of four bases called adenine (A), cytosine (C), guanine (G) and thymine (T). Millions of nucleotides link up to make each DNA molecule. The deoxyribose and phosphate groups form a 'backbone' on the outside.

◄ Chromosomes are found in the cell's nucleus. Each one is made up of a DNA double helix that is coiled up, then coiled again into a supercoil – a bit like a telephone cord – which is held together by proteins.

▲ This 'typical' cell (see pages 12–13), which has a central nucleus, surrounded by a jelly-like cytoplasm bounded by a thin cell membrane, is controlled by the DNA inside its nucleus.

▲ The bases – A, C, G and T – hold the strands together, like rungs on a ladder. Notice that the bases always form specific pairs – each can only pair with the same partner. A always pairs with T, and C always pairs with G.

The double helix

O ur cells contain a set of operating instructions in the form of deoxyribonucleic acid, or DNA. DNA always has the same basic structure – two long strands that wind around each other to form a double helix, or spiral. DNA holds the coded instructions, called genes, that are needed to build and run cells. Importantly, it can also copy itself, making sure that instructions are passed on accurately when cells divide.

DNA's structure

The 46 chromosomes inside the nucleus of each human body cell contain an incredible two metres of DNA in total. Each long, thin DNA double helix is made up of building blocks called nucleotides. Each nucleotide consists of a sugar called deoxyribose, another component called a phosphate group, and one of four 'letters' or bases. Millions of nucleotides link up to make each DNA molecule. The molecule looks like a twisted ladder with the bases acting as 'rungs'.

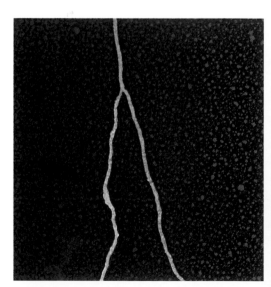

▲ This electron micrograph shows, under high magnification, a DNA molecule actually in the process of replication – unzipping and copying itself. Each new DNA double helix consists of one old strand and one new one.

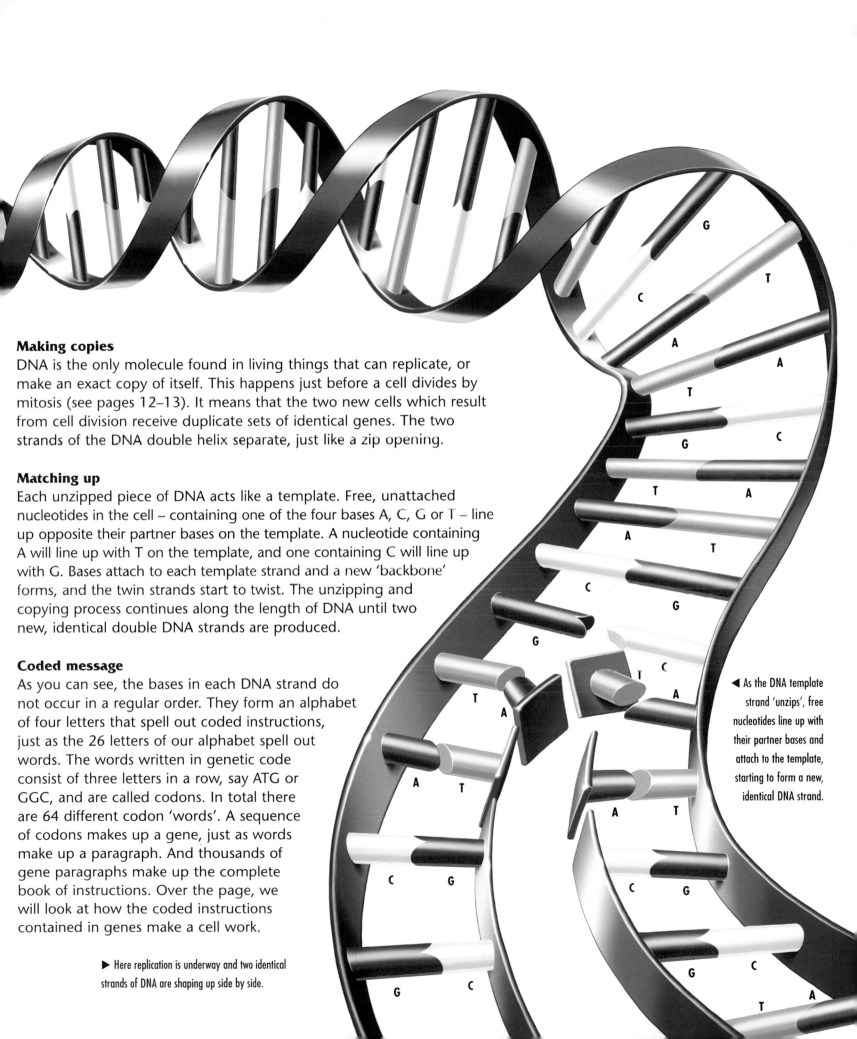

Making copies

DNA is the only molecule found in living things that can replicate, or make an exact copy of itself. This happens just before a cell divides by mitosis (see pages 12–13). It means that the two new cells which result from cell division receive duplicate sets of identical genes. The two strands of the DNA double helix separate, just like a zip opening.

Matching up

Each unzipped piece of DNA acts like a template. Free, unattached nucleotides in the cell – containing one of the four bases A, C, G or T – line up opposite their partner bases on the template. A nucleotide containing A will line up with T on the template, and one containing C will line up with G. Bases attach to each template strand and a new 'backbone' forms, and the twin strands start to twist. The unzipping and copying process continues along the length of DNA until two new, identical double DNA strands are produced.

Coded message

As you can see, the bases in each DNA strand do not occur in a regular order. They form an alphabet of four letters that spell out coded instructions, just as the 26 letters of our alphabet spell out words. The words written in genetic code consist of three letters in a row, say ATG or GGC, and are called codons. In total there are 64 different codon 'words'. A sequence of codons makes up a gene, just as words make up a paragraph. And thousands of gene paragraphs make up the complete book of instructions. Over the page, we will look at how the coded instructions contained in genes make a cell work.

◄ As the DNA template strand 'unzips', free nucleotides line up with their partner bases and attach to the template, starting to form a new, identical DNA strand.

▶ Here replication is underway and two identical strands of DNA are shaping up side by side.

DNA at work

In earlier pages, we have seen how genes, which determine our features and carry them from one generation to the next, are made of DNA. Now, we reach the exciting moment when we can see how genes actually work. The DNA in genes controls the production of substances called proteins. These, in turn, build our bodies and run our cells. The mechanism by which DNA's coded message is used to make proteins is present in the cells of all living things.

RNA molecule

DNA molecule

What are proteins?

Just about everything in your body is either made by, or made of, chemicals called proteins. Some proteins make cells work. Enzymes, for example, speed up the chemical reactions inside cells that produce things or release the energy cells need to stay alive. Other proteins form structures such as hair, skin and muscles. Proteins are made up of building blocks called amino acids. There are 20 different types of amino acids. Each type of protein is made up of its own set of amino acids, joined together in a chain in a specific order. That order is determined by a set of coded instructions – a gene – stored in the DNA double helix.

Copying the message

As we have seen, chromosomes are found inside the nucleus of a cell. Proteins are made in the cell's cytoplasm, the jelly-like bit that surrounds the nucleus. So how do the instructions contained inside a gene get to the place where proteins are made? DNA molecules are too big to get through the pores (holes) in the nuclear membrane. What happens instead is that the short section of DNA containing a particular gene is copied into a very close relative of DNA called RNA (ribonucleic acid). RNA has just one strand, not two like DNA. It has three of the same 'letters' as DNA – adenine (A), cytosine (C) and guanine (G) – but its fourth 'letter' is not thymine (T) but uracil (U). The diagram (left) shows how copying, called transcription, happens.

◄ When a gene is copied, first the stretch of DNA containing that gene 'unzips', just like it does during replication (see pages 28–29). Then, free RNA nucleotides line up with the unzipped section, pairing up with matching bases on one of the DNA strands. The bases link up to form an RNA strand called messenger RNA or mRNA. Once it has copied the message contained in the gene, the mRNA molecule travels through a hole in the nuclear membrane and into the cytoplasm, ready for the next stage in the process.

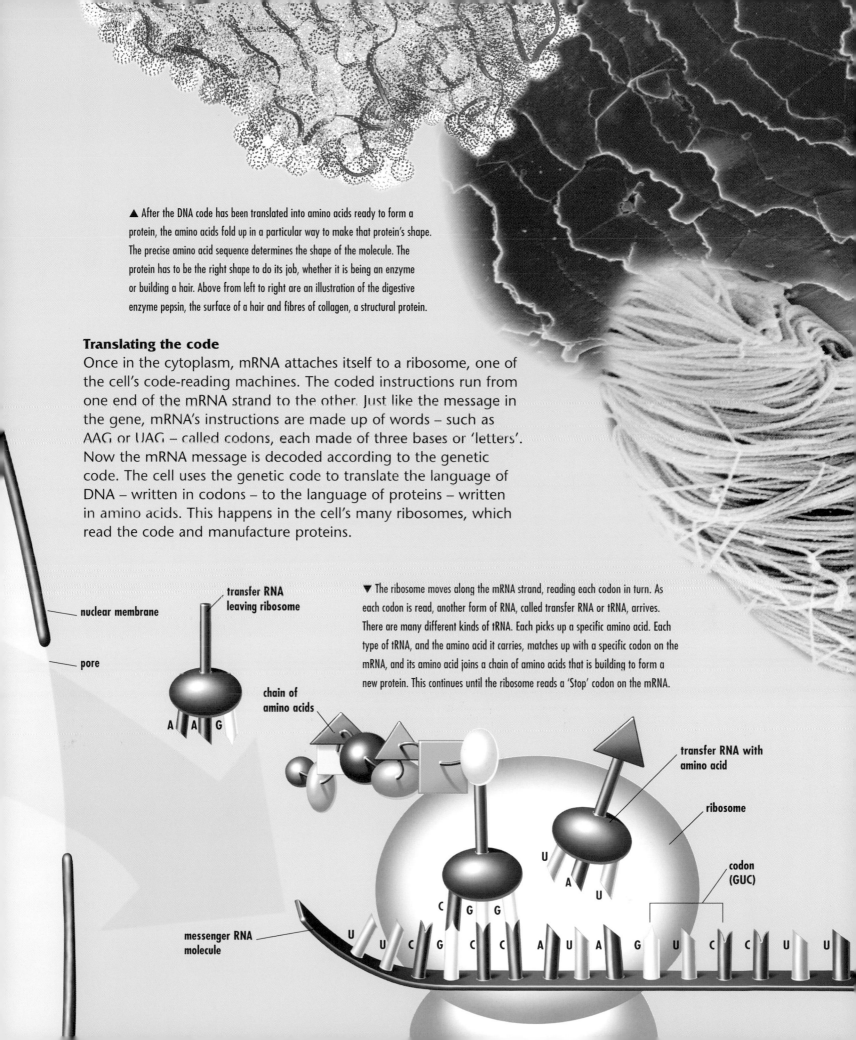

▲ After the DNA code has been translated into amino acids ready to form a protein, the amino acids fold up in a particular way to make that protein's shape. The precise amino acid sequence determines the shape of the molecule. The protein has to be the right shape to do its job, whether it is being an enzyme or building a hair. Above from left to right are an illustration of the digestive enzyme pepsin, the surface of a hair and fibres of collagen, a structural protein.

Translating the code

Once in the cytoplasm, mRNA attaches itself to a ribosome, one of the cell's code-reading machines. The coded instructions run from one end of the mRNA strand to the other. Just like the message in the gene, mRNA's instructions are made up of words – such as AAG or UAG – called codons, each made of three bases or 'letters'. Now the mRNA message is decoded according to the genetic code. The cell uses the genetic code to translate the language of DNA – written in codons – to the language of proteins – written in amino acids. This happens in the cell's many ribosomes, which read the code and manufacture proteins.

transfer RNA
leaving ribosome

nuclear membrane

pore

chain of
amino acids

A A G

▼ The ribosome moves along the mRNA strand, reading each codon in turn. As each codon is read, another form of RNA, called transfer RNA or tRNA, arrives. There are many different kinds of tRNA. Each picks up a specific amino acid. Each type of tRNA, and the amino acid it carries, matches up with a specific codon on the mRNA, and its amino acid joins a chain of amino acids that is building to form a new protein. This continues until the ribosome reads a 'Stop' codon on the mRNA.

transfer RNA with
amino acid

ribosome

codon
(GUC)

messenger RNA
molecule

U U C G C C A U A G U C C U U

Changing the message

DNA holds the set of instructions that controls a cell. But sometimes tiny changes, called mutations, happen to those instructions. Mutations may be caused by faulty copying, or by outside factors such as radiation. By changing DNA's coded instructions, mutations may alter the proteins that are produced by these instructions. This may have a harmful effect, no effect at all, or even a beneficial effect. Let's look at some examples of the effect of mutations, and then see how they happen.

Sickle cell disease

Our blood contains billions of red blood cells. They are packed with the protein haemoglobin, which carries life-giving oxygen to all of our body cells. A mutation in the gene that produces haemoglobin changes one of its amino acid building blocks. This small change alters the shape of haemoglobin molecules. This in turn can change the shape of the red blood cell so it becomes sickle shaped (curved). Sickle cells can block blood vessels, causing muscle cramps and shortness of breath. If just one partner in a pair of alleles is abnormal, there is little effect on blood cells. But if both alleles are abnormal, sickle cell disease is much more serious.

▲ Blood taken from someone without sickle cell disease contains only normal doughnut-shaped red blood cells (top). Blood taken from someone with the condition (above) contains normal cells and the different-looking, sickle-shaped red blood cells.

Clotting problems

Another problem affecting the blood also involves a gene mutation. If we cut ourselves, chemicals in the blood cause it to clot, so that bleeding stops. But, very rarely, a mutation occurs that produces a defective version of a clotting chemical called factor VIII. This causes an illness called haemophilia. A person with haemophilia carries on bleeding when cut and might eventually die. Fortunately, haemophilia can be treated today using injections of working factor VIII. The mutant allele for haemophilia is carried on an X chromosome (see pages 18–19), so it is usually only males who get haemophilia.

Royal inheritance

A famous example of haemophilia happened in the royal families of Europe. Britain's Queen Victoria, although not a sufferer herself, was a carrier of the haemophilia allele, produced by a mutation on an X chromosome in her father's sperm or mother's egg. Victoria's daughter Alice inherited the mutant allele and passed it on to her daughter Alexandra, who married Tsar Nicholas II of Russia. Their son, Tsarevitch Alexis, inherited the allele and suffered from haemophilia. Alexis' parents sought help from a holy man called Rasputin, who relieved Alexis' painful symptoms. Because of his importance to the tsarevitch, Rasputin had great influence over the royal family and caused them to make some bad decisions. The tsar and his family were murdered in 1918, following the Russian Revolution (see pages 42–43).

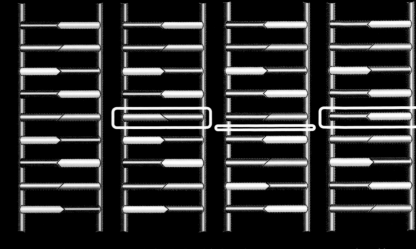

▲ On the left is a 'normal' strand of DNA. The other three show various mutations, as indicated by the boxes. On the second strand, a substitution has occurred, changing a base pair. On the third strand, a deletion has occurred, removing a base pair. On the fourth strand, an insertion has occurred so there is an extra base pair in the sequence. These mutations can cause changes in amino acid sequences.

Misunderstandings

There are various ways that mutations change the genetic message. The diagram above shows how these work, but we can also show this by imagining what the same changes would do to the meaning of a message written in English. The commonest mutation is caused by a substitution which changes just one 'letter' or base in the DNA. So, for example, the original sentence THE CAT SAT ON THE MAT would become THE CAR SAT ON THE MAT – a completely different meaning. Sometimes a base is missed out or deleted. So ASK FRIEND TO COLLECT CAT becomes ASK FIEND TO COLLECT CAT. Or a base can be inserted. The message PLEASE PUT THE CAT OUT becomes PLEASE PUT THE CART OUT. In the case of substitution, the commonest mutation, a DNA codon is changed, and if it codes for an amino acid, that may be changed as well. With deletions and insertions, neighbouring codons are altered, and this may stop a gene from producing a protein at all.

◄ Shown here is the Russian royal family – Tsar Nicholas II and his wife, their four daughters and the tsarevitch Alexis (second from right), who suffered from haemophilia. Rasputin (inset) was a monk who greatly influenced the family while treating the tsarevitch. Some say that without Alexis' haemophilia – and Rasputin's bad influence – the Russian Revolution would never have happened.

Human Genome Project

In April 1953, James Watson and Francis Crick worked out the structure of DNA. Fifty years later, in April 2003, scientists working on the Human Genome Project had succeeded in reading the sequence of bases in the DNA in human cells. They had worked out the order of the 'letters' – A, C, G and T – which make up the coded messages of genes. These coded messages, in turn, control how our bodies are assembled and how they work, and can determine whether we suffer from certain diseases.

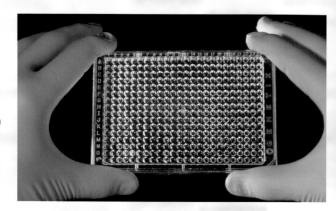

▼ The photograph below was taken at the Sanger Centre in Cambridge, England, one of the 16 research centres involved in the HGP. A researcher holds a tray with 384 tiny 'wells'. Each well contains a different piece of copied human DNA, ready to be sequenced.

What is the human genome?

As we have seen, the DNA in a human cell is contained in two sets of 22 ordinary chromosomes and two sex chromosomes – XX or XY. The human genome is all the DNA in one complete set of chromosomes 1 to 22, plus both of the sex chromosomes, making 24 in all. The aim of the Human Genome Project (HGP) is firstly to find out the precise sequence of bases A, C, G and T in the DNA molecules that make up a genome, and secondly to make a complete map of the genome, showing which genes are found where.

First steps

An easy task? No! The genome of just one human cell is an incredible one metre long and is made up of millions of pairs of bases (A paired with T and G paired with C). That is why the Human Genome Project, which started in 1990, needed the combined efforts of thousands of scientists in 16 research institutes in six countries. The early stages involved making 'maps' of chromosomes to pinpoint the location of certain genes. Later, these maps would help scientists match the message (sequence of bases) to a particular gene. But the key part of the HGP was sequencing DNA.

Sequencing DNA

DNA molecules are very long and thin. So that scientists can work out the precise order of bases that make up its messages, they need to cut DNA into smaller pieces of different lengths. These bits of DNA are then sequenced automatically, and the base sequences are 'read' by a computer. This looks for patterns and puts the pieces of the DNA jigsaw back together again. At first this process was slow. But as the project advanced – with new machines and more powerful computers – it got faster. Today, 1,000 base pairs can be sequenced every second.

◀ Seen here under a microscope, the roundworm *Caenorhabditis elegans* is just one millimetre long. Scientists working on the HGP sequenced its genome (97 million base pairs) and those of other simple organisms, to help them make sense of the much larger human genome.

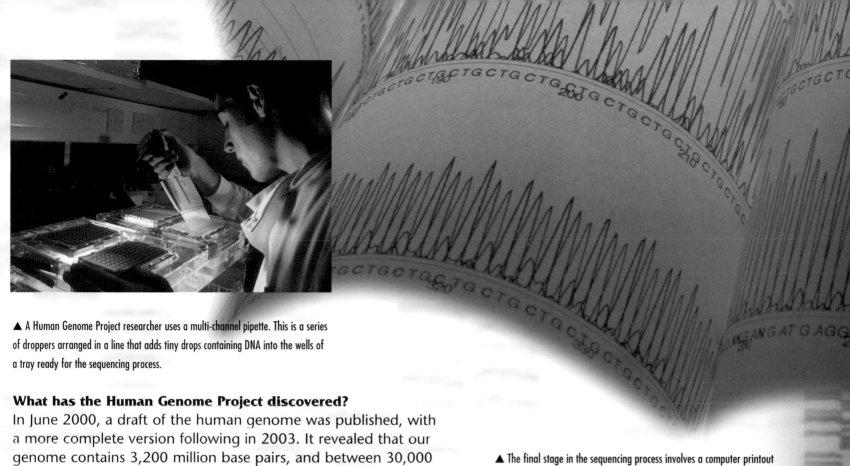

▲ A Human Genome Project researcher uses a multi-channel pipette. This is a series of droppers arranged in a line that adds tiny drops containing DNA into the wells of a tray ready for the sequencing process.

What has the Human Genome Project discovered?

In June 2000, a draft of the human genome was published, with a more complete version following in 2003. It revealed that our genome contains 3,200 million base pairs, and between 30,000 and 40,000 genes, far fewer than the 100,000 expected. Amazingly, genes take up just three per cent of DNA. The rest – called 'junk' DNA – does not code for proteins or control other genes. It serves as a record of what has happened during human evolution, including invasion by bacteria and viruses.

▲ The final stage in the sequencing process involves a computer printout like this one. It shows the sequence of bases, or 'letters', in one piece of DNA. By putting information about all these pieces together, scientists can 'read' the whole genome.

Tiny differences and future developments

The HGP has also shown that the base sequences of any two genomes are 99.9 per cent identical. That is why we all look so similar. But 0.1 per cent of the 3.2 billion bases (about one base in every 1,000) differs. For example, ...ATTACGGT... in one person's genome might be ...ATTCCGGT... in the same section of another. These are single base changes and occur mainly in 'junk' DNA. But the changes that occur in genes are what makes us individuals, including whether we have, or may get, certain diseases. Understanding how our genome affects our health will be of vital importance in years to come. So will finding out the sequence of individual genes, what proteins these genes produce, and how they work inside a cell.

▼ Stored in a laboratory refrigerator, these labelled tubes each contain a particular section of human DNA. Together they hold a complete human genome. A store like this is called a DNA library.

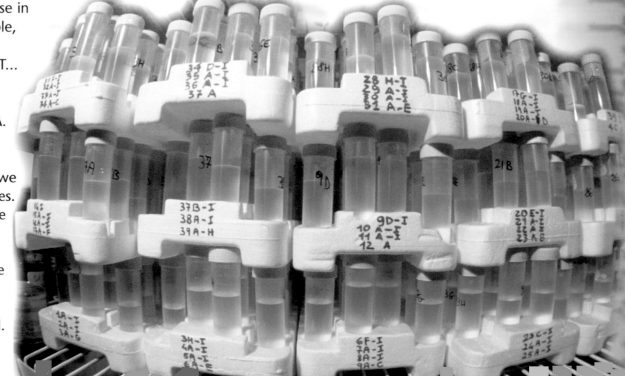

DNA, genes and evolution

There are well over a million species of living organisms on earth. Millions more existed once but have died out. All these species arose by evolution, a gradual process of change that occurs over many generations. Evolution gives rise to new species and ensures that they are adapted, or suited, to their surroundings. English scientist Charles Darwin was the first to explain evolution in the 19th century. More recent discoveries of genes and DNA have supported his ideas.

▲ Naturalist Charles Darwin published his theory of evolution in 1859, having spent over 20 years putting together the evidence to support his ideas.

Voyage of discovery

Between 1831 and 1836, Charles Darwin was the naturalist on board the Royal Navy ship *HMS Beagle*. During a round-the-world voyage, Darwin made expeditions on land to study the natural history of South America, and of a group of islands in the Pacific Ocean called the Galápagos. Darwin noticed that many species of animals on the islands were unique to the Galápagos and found nowhere else. But he also found that they showed similarities to animals found in South America, some 1,000km across the ocean. Why should this be so?

Darwin's theory

Darwin suggested that the Galápagos were volcanic islands that had erupted as bare rocks from the ocean floor. In time, certain animals arrived from mainland South America having flown, been blown, or floated to the islands. Here, the new arrivals found living conditions very different. Over time, species changed, or evolved, as they adapted to their new environment, until after a few million years they no longer resembled their relatives in South America. Darwin proposed that all species on earth had arisen in the same way by evolution, with species arising gradually from other species.

▼ *HMS Beagle* was the survey ship that carried the young Charles Darwin on his voyage around the world, during which he gained his first ideas about evolution.

▲ Giant tortoises like this one gave the Galápagos Islands their name (*galápago* is the Spanish for tortoise). They have evolved to exist in different forms on different islands, related to their feeding habits.

◄ These heads and beaks are of four of the 13 species of finches found on the Galápagos Islands and nowhere else. Each of the 13 species has a differently shaped beak. The size and shape of the beak is related to what each finch eats. The finch at the top, for example, has a large beak for crushing big seeds. The others eat insects, leaves or cacti. Darwin noticed the variety of finches on the Galápagos and suggested that they had evolved from a single species of seed-eating finch that had flown there from South America millions of years ago.

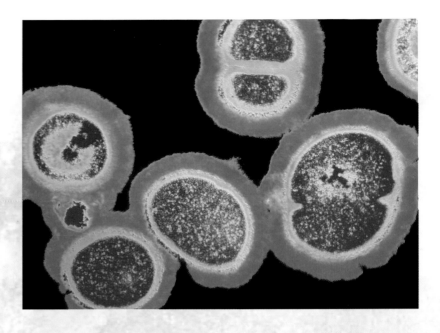

▲ This is MRSA, an example of evolution in action today. This new and deadly form of the disease-causing bacterium *Staphylococcus aureus* has appeared recently and is resistant to most antibiotics, the drugs used to kill bacteria. Normally evolution is too slow to observe, but bacteria reproduce very rapidly.

Natural selection

Darwin based his theory on three observations: variation, inheritance and competition. Variation occurs within all species of living things. Inheritance means that parents pass their features to their offspring. Competition among living things is fierce for resources such as food, water, shelter and mates. Darwin proposed that some individuals within a species show variations that enable them to compete more effectively than others. These individuals are more likely to survive, breed, and pass on their useful features to their offspring. This process, called natural selection, is the driving force of evolution. Over many generations, natural selection can produce changes that result in a new species. The discovery of genes and DNA added to our understanding of evolution.

Modern DNA evidence

We now know that features are inherited from parents through genes, and that mutations, or changes, in those genes produce variation. Scientists have found that mutations are caused by accidental changes in DNA. What's more, the fact that living things use the same genetic code suggests they have all, humans included, evolved from a common ancestor that existed billions of years ago. Comparing genes from different species also reveals how closely related they are. Humans share 99.9 per cent of their genes with other humans, 98.5 per cent with chimpanzees, 90 per cent with mice, and even 7 per cent with bacteria.

◄ The Galápagos flightless cormorant is a bird that, over millions of years in a habitat with no natural enemies, lost its ability to fly.

▼ Galápagos marine iguanas are the only lizards in the world that swim and feed in the sea. They evolved from land-living iguanas that probably floated to the Galápagos from South America on uprooted trees or other vegetation millions of years ago.

SUMMARY OF CHAPTER 2: DNA: THE MOLECULE OF LIFE

The secret of life

It had already been known for some years that DNA was the molecule of which genes are made, when two young scientists, James Watson and Francis Crick, took on the challenge of working out its structure. In 1953, they constructed a model which showed that each DNA molecule consisted of two long chains that spiralled around each other in a twisted ladder shape – a double helix.

Other scientists soon confirmed that they had, as Crick described it, discovered the 'secret of life'. DNA carries the instructions needed to construct and operate a complete human being, or any other living thing. In Chapter 2, we have seen how it does this by looking at its structure. The sequence of bases – A, C, G and T – running along the length of a section of DNA – a gene – carry the instructions needed to make a

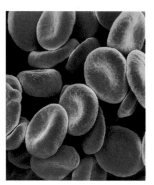

Red blood cells – one of the human body's hundreds of different types of cells

protein. By making proteins, which build and run cells, DNA controls an organism's features.

Reading the sequence

DNA is unique in its ability to copy itself. This means that when cells divide, each new daughter cell has a complete set of genetic instructions. Most of the time, copying ensures that the instructions are passed on exactly when cells divide or when transcription happens. But copying is not always perfect, and mistakes, called mutations, occur. Most are harmless, but some can cause diseases and may be passed on to the next generation. Looking for mutations, which cause variations between people, was one of the aims of the Human Genome Project. This massive project used the latest technology to read the sequence of bases along the DNA in a set of human chromosomes – the human genome.

The variation produced by differences in DNA between one individual organism and another affects many things about their life, including their chances of survival. Over millions of years, these variations have allowed living things to gradually change, or evolve.

Go further...

Crack the code of life with a journey into DNA and more at: www.pbs.org/wgbh/nova/genome

Get the inside information on the Human Genome Project at: www.yourgenome.org

Take an on-line quiz about genes and evolution at: www.vilenski.org/science/notebook/unit2/index.html

Find out lots more about DNA at: www.eurekascience.com/ICanDoThat/index.htm

The Kingfisher Book of Evolution by Stephen Webster (Kingfisher, 2000)

Biochemist
Studies the way in which chemicals react inside living things.

Molecular biologist
Uses modern technology to study complex chemicals, such as DNA, that are found in living things.

Bioinformatician
Combines biology with mathematics and computer science to analyze the structure of biological systems, using information from, for example, the Human Genome Project.

Evolutionary biologist
Studies living things, researching their evolution and the relationships between them.

Visit the Traits of Life Exhibition at San Francisco's Exploratorium: www.exploratorium.edu
3601 Lyon Street,
San Francisco CA
USA
T: 001 (415) 561-0308

Visit Charles Darwin's house and see where he worked on his theory of evolution:
Down House,
Luxted Road,
Downe,
Kent BR6 7JK
T: 01689 859119

CHAPTER 3

Genetic technology

A science technician gazes at a DNA fingerprint, its patterns unique to an individual person. This is just one of the many techniques and developments that have been made possible by genetic technology, applying our understanding of DNA to improve our health and well-being. Gene science already has many applications in everyday life. Genetic engineering, gene therapy, cloning and DNA profiling are all happening right now. But what of the future? Will we know what our genes hold in store for us, as far as diseases are concerned? Should we be able to select certain genes in order to 'design' our own children? Will genetic technology really allow us to live better lives, or will it raise a host of new problems?

This 'ordinary' fingerprint is made up of a unique pattern produced by ridges on the fingertips.

DNA fingerprinting

Our fingertips are covered with tiny ridges that leave behind sweaty patterns – fingerprints – when we touch things. Individual fingerprints are unique, and not shared with anyone else. Police can use fingerprints left at the scene of a crime to identify and convict criminals. Today, detectives have a more sophisticated way of catching crooks – by identifying their unique DNA 'fingerprints'.

Gathering evidence

Whoever robbed this office thought they were being clever. By wearing gloves, they left no fingerprints. But a specially trained officer discovered something interesting. As the thief left, his or her head snagged against the broken window, pulling out some hairs. The officer carefully collected the hairs and sent them to a forensic laboratory. Here, scientists extracted the DNA from cells in the base of the hairs to make a DNA fingerprint that would pinpoint one of three people under suspicion.

► A broken window, disturbed office furniture, and belongings stolen. The thief has long since departed this crime scene. But has he, or she, left behind any traces that can be used for DNA fingerprinting?

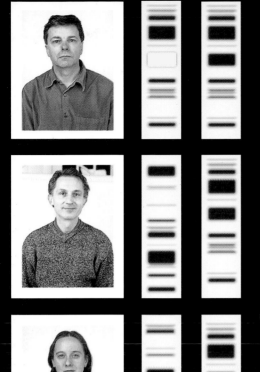

◄ These suspects have been arrested. A police surgeon has taken blood samples from each of them. Forensic scientists have used cells from the blood to produce DNA fingerprints. Here, each DNA fingerprint is shown next to the suspect it belongs to, with the fingerprint from the hair found at the crime scene next to each for comparison.

▼ A strand of hair provides the vital evidence in this crime. Cells taken from the hair roots are used to prepare a DNA fingerprint that can be compared with the suspects' DNA.

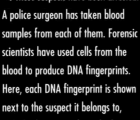

Making a DNA fingerprint

The three per cent of our DNA involved with building our bodies (see pages 34–35) is virtually the same in all of us. But the remaining 97 per cent, the so-called 'junk' DNA, has sections that vary a lot between people. These sections consist of stretches of DNA code that repeat themselves between five and 1,000 times, and are dotted throughout the genome. The number of repeats in each of these sections, and therefore its size, varies a lot from one person to another. Scientists can break up a person's DNA, pick out the repeated sections, and separate them by size, to produce a special photograph that looks like a barcode. This DNA fingerprint is unique for that person.

Conclusive proof?

So, who burgled the office? Have a look at the evidence presented left and match up the DNA fingerprint produced from the hair sample with one of the suspects' DNA fingerprints. The evidence is conclusive – it was the man (top photo). Or is it? Not if he has an identical twin, with an identical genome. But otherwise, there is only a minuscule chance that someone else would have the same DNA fingerprint. DNA fingerprinting has solved many real-life crimes, resulting in the conviction of criminals and proving the innocence of people who have been wrongly accused.

▼ Forensic scientists, seen here examining DNA fingerprints, specialize in examining evidence from crime scenes in order to help police arrest and convict criminals. Using modern techniques, they can extract enough DNA to make a fingerprint from just a tiny flake of skin, drop of blood or drop of saliva.

Tracing ancestors

Where do we come from? Who were our ancestors tens, hundreds or even thousands of years ago? Answers to these fascinating questions are coming from DNA technology. Our DNA carries evidence of ancestry from centuries past, so scientists are now using the small differences between the DNA in each of us to trace ancestors both recent and ancient. They use DNA found in two particular locations in our cells – in the Y chromosome of males and in mitochondria.

DNA detectives

DNA is unique in being able to copy itself. But the copying process is not always perfect, and sometimes mistakes, or mutations, happen. If mutations are inherited, they can be detected. So, can mutations act as markers to trace ancestry? Generally, no, because every time humans reproduce, each offspring gets half his or her DNA from each parent (see pages 14–15). Over time, markers get shuffled. That is where the Y chromosome and mitochondria come in useful. Their DNA – including mutations – passes unshuffled from one generation to the next.

From father to son

Our 23 pairs of chromosomes include the sex chromosomes (see pages 18–19) – XX in females and XY in males. When cells in a man's testes divide to make sperm, their 22 pairs of ordinary chromosomes swap bits of DNA between them before they separate. But the Y chromosome does not swap bits of DNA with its 'partner', the X sex chromosome. The DNA in the Y chromosome passes unchanged down the male line from father to son.

Out of Africa

Y chromosomes do contain some mutations, though, and these build up over time. Scientists have compared markers in the Y chromosomes of males around the world, so they can work out where humans first came from. By comparing DNA markers that are more common around the world (older) with those that are less common (newer), scientists have been able to construct a male family tree. This provides evidence to support the theory that humans first evolved in Africa. Some humans migrated out of Africa over 60,000 years ago and spread to all of the world's continents (except Antarctica) within the next 50,000 years.

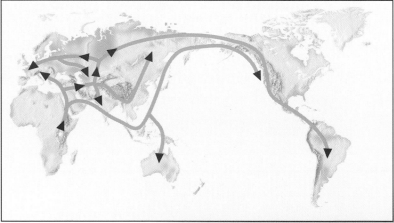

◄◄ Based on evidence from Y chromosomes, the map traces how humans spread around the world after leaving Africa over 60,000 years ago. They reached Australia about 55,000 years ago, Asia 45,000 years ago, Europe 35,000 years ago and the Americas about 15,000 years ago.

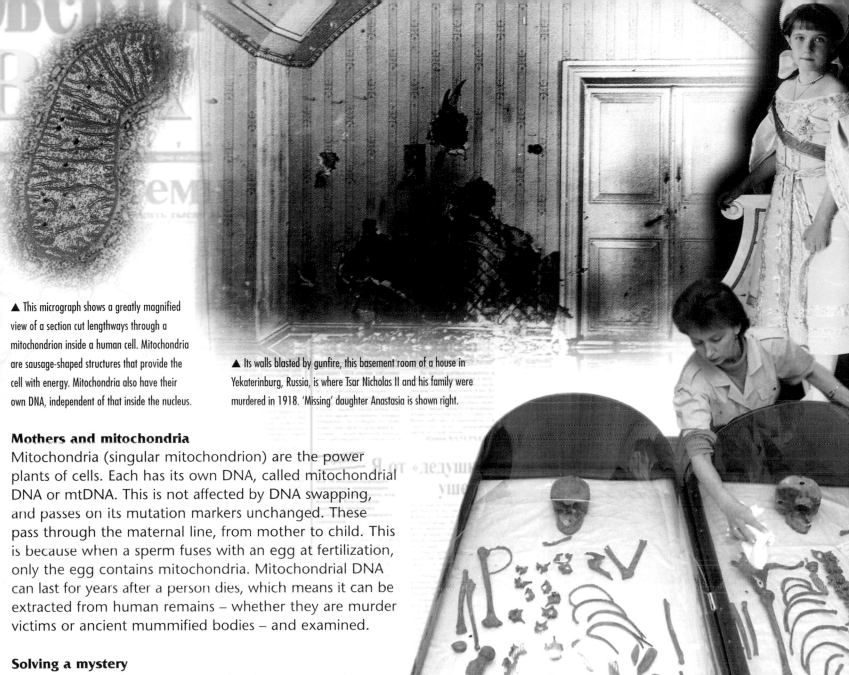

▲ This micrograph shows a greatly magnified view of a section cut lengthways through a mitochondrion inside a human cell. Mitochondria are sausage-shaped structures that provide the cell with energy. Mitochondria also have their own DNA, independent of that inside the nucleus.

▲ Its walls blasted by gunfire, this basement room of a house in Yekaterinburg, Russia, is where Tsar Nicholas II and his family were murdered in 1918. 'Missing' daughter Anastasia is shown right.

Mothers and mitochondria

Mitochondria (singular mitochondrion) are the power plants of cells. Each has its own DNA, called mitochondrial DNA or mtDNA. This is not affected by DNA swapping, and passes on its mutation markers unchanged. These pass through the maternal line, from mother to child. This is because when a sperm fuses with an egg at fertilization, only the egg contains mitochondria. Mitochondrial DNA can last for years after a person dies, which means it can be extracted from human remains – whether they are murder victims or ancient mummified bodies – and examined.

Solving a mystery

A famous case where mtDNA technology was used to trace ancestors is that of the Russian royal family. After the Russian Revolution in 1917, the tsar, Nicholas II, and his family were murdered. Their bodies disappeared. When the remains were discovered in 1991, mtDNA technology was used

◄ Walking across a grassland in southwestern Africa, these are San people. Evidence from their Y chromosomes shows that they belong to one of the oldest human populations on earth, and provide us with a direct link to our earliest ancestors.

to prove their identity, by comparing the remains with living members of the same family. Scientists in England took a blood sample from Prince Philip, husband of Queen Elizabeth II and related through the maternal line to the tsar's wife Alexandra (she was his grandmother's sister). His mtDNA matched mtDNA taken from one of the nine sets of bones, proving that they were the remains of Alexandra. More tests showed that three of the skeletons belong to Alexandra's daughters. The tests also solved another mystery. In 1920, a woman called Anna Anderson had claimed she was the tsar's daughter Anastasia and that she had escaped execution. Many people, including some relatives of the murdered family, believed her. But mtDNA analysis proved that she was not Anastasia.

▲ These skeletal remains, laid out in a mortuary in Yekaterinburg, were believed to be those of Tsar Nicholas II and his family. Analysis of mtDNA taken from the bones showed this to be true. The remains were buried in St Petersburg Cathedral on 17 July 1998, exactly 80 years after the murders.

Genetic engineering

For thousands of years, people have slowly altered animals and plants, by selective breeding, to produce the pets, farm animals and crops they needed. But today, scientists can change an organism's features much faster, by altering its genes through a process called genetic engineering. Their aim is to produce genetically modified (GM) organisms that provide improved food or that benefit human health. Not everyone agrees that this is a good thing, however.

▲ These tomatoes have been stored under the same conditions. Two are going mouldy. The other three are mould-free, because a mould-resistance gene was introduced by genetic engineering into the plant that produced them.

New genes

Genetic engineering alters an organism's DNA. Usually it is done by introducing a new gene from another organism of a completely different species. This would normally be impossible, because different species cannot breed with each other. But genetic engineering makes the impossible possible. How? First, scientists find an organism with the 'useful' gene that produces a desired feature. Then they use chemical 'scissors' to cut out the gene. Finally, they insert it into the DNA of the other organism. They either smuggle the gene into the organism's cells using a carrier virus or bacterium – as with the jellyfish gene introduced into the fertilized eggs that produced the glowing mice (right) – or push it in using a special 'gun' or injector.

▼ A farm worker in Java, Indonesia, tends a crop of rice in a paddy field. Rice is a staple food for half the world's population, including many of the planet's poorest people, who depend on this vital crop to keep them alive.

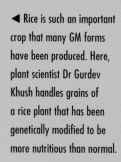

◄ Rice is such an important crop that many GM forms have been produced. Here, plant scientist Dr Gurdev Khush handles grains of a rice plant that has been genetically modified to be more nutritious than normal.

Genetically modified salmon can grow twice as fast as 'normal' salmon. GM fish could provide an affordable source of protein, especially for people with poor diets.

GM organisms

Imagine taking a gene from an Arctic fish, which produces an 'antifreeze' protein that stops its blood from freezing, and inserting it into a strawberry to make it frost-resistant. Or putting a human gene into bacteria so they produce insulin to treat people with diabetes, a disease caused by a lack of insulin, a hormone normally made by the body to control levels of glucose (sugar) in the blood. This is not science fiction. These GM organisms already exist, and many more are planned. They include GM bananas which produce a vaccine against cholera, and GM plants that make plastics. But many of today's GM organisms are food crops.

Bug-free maize and golden rice

Let's consider two GM crops. Corn (maize) is attacked by the corn borer caterpillar. Scientists discovered that a bacterium called *Bacillus thuringiensis* (Bt) makes poisons that kill pests like the corn borer. So they took the genes that make the poisons and inserted them into corn to produce Bt corn, with its own built-in pesticide. No need, therefore, to spray plants with expensive, polluting pesticides. Rice is a staple food for billions of people, but it lacks the vital nutrient vitamin A. Scientists took a daffodil gene that produces beta-carotene – which the human body turns into vitamin A – and inserted it into rice plants. The result is golden rice, which contains beta-carotene and, therefore, provides vitamin A.

◄ These baby mice have been given a jellyfish gene that makes their skin glow green under a blue light. This gene may help in the study of cancer.

▼ Many people feel strongly that GM organisms may harm the environment. Here, an anti-GM protestor, later arrested by police, destroys GM crops and collects samples at an experimental farm in England, one of several countries where anti-GM protests have taken place.

For or against?

Since the first genetic engineering experiments in the 1970s, the use of GM organisms has provoked fierce arguments. On one side, people argue that GM organisms will be vital to feed the world and ensure increasing health and prosperity. Others argue that swapping genes between species could have unforeseen and serious effects on our health and environment. Bt corn, for example, may kill harmless butterflies and other insects. It could potentially lead to the evolution of superbugs resistant to its poisons. Others are concerned that the companies that produce GM organisms will have too much control over the world's resources. The arguments continue.

Screening for diseases

Tiny changes, or mutations, in the DNA in our genes can affect our health by causing diseases. These faulty genes may be inherited by the next generation. Scientists can now screen people for certain inherited diseases. One day there may be a full range of genetic tests to tell us whether we are at risk from serious illnesses, and what we can do to reduce the risk of becoming ill.

▲ A physiotherapist uses a flow meter to measure how well this girl's lungs are working. She suffers from an inherited disease called cystic fibrosis, which can block tubes inside the lungs.

▼ A tiny prick to this newborn baby's heel, and drops of blood are squeezed onto a special test card that will indicate whether or not it has the inherited disease PKU.

At birth

The PKU test is a blood test given to all newborn babies. It does not spot a faulty gene, but identifies the problem it causes, brought on by an inherited disease called phenylketonuria (PKU), which affects one child in every 10,000. The test detects high levels in the blood of an amino acid (see pages 30–31) called phenylalanine, which we get from proteins in our food. PKU is caused by a faulty gene that fails to produce the enzyme which normally breaks down phenylalanine. This can build up in the blood and cause brain damage. Luckily, testing at birth can mean the problems are prevented. If a child has PKU, he or she is put on a special diet and will not become ill.

Genetic counselling

If parents-to-be are worried that they might pass on inherited diseases, such as cystic fibrosis, to their children, they can have genetic counselling. Caused by a single gene, cystic fibrosis affects mainly white children (about one in 2,500). It makes their body fluids thicker than normal. If parents suspect they might carry the faulty gene, found on chromosome 7, this can be tested. If both parents are carriers they can find out how likely it is that their child will have cystic fibrosis, and what the implications of the child having the disease might be.

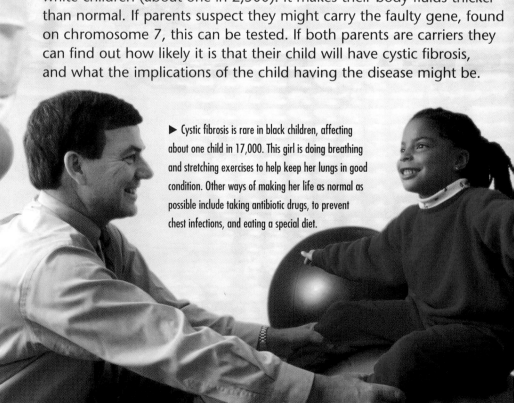

▶ Cystic fibrosis is rare in black children, affecting about one child in 17,000. This girl is doing breathing and stretching exercises to help keep her lungs in good condition. Other ways of making her life as normal as possible include taking antibiotic drugs, to prevent chest infections, and eating a special diet.

► A doctor looks at an ECG (electrocardiogram), which records the pattern produced when the electrical signal that causes each heartbeat passes through the heart. The shape of the ECG trace tells her whether or not the patient's heart is working properly.

Detect and treat

Some inherited diseases may be caused by a number of genes. That is what scientists are trying to discover about a rare inherited heart condition called long QT syndrome, that affects about one in 5,000 people. This can cause an upset in the heart's natural rhythm which can make someone pass out or even die. Until recently, families affected did not know why they were suffering the loss of family members to sudden death at quite a young age. Scientists still do not know which gene or genes cause long QT, but it can now be detected by testing the heart with an ECG, and treated by putting a pacemaker in the chest. This picks up unusual heartbeats, and gives the heart an electric shock to jolt it back to normal.

▲ This man is 'wired up' to an ECG while walking on a treadmill. The pads on his chest pick up electrical signals from his heart and pass them on to the ECG machine, being monitored by the doctor. Walking puts the heart under more stress than when the body is at rest, and can show up problems on an ECG trace that are not noticeable when a person is sitting down.

Reducing the risks

Both PKU and cystic fibrosis are caused by defects in a single gene. But for most diseases it is not as simple as that. We all have some faulty genes, and it may be that any one of them can make us more likely to develop certain common diseases such as allergies or heart disease. But simply having the genes does not necessarily mean we will get the disease. In many cases our lifestyles also contribute to our developing certain conditions. So, for example, someone who has an inherited tendency to heart disease could reduce their risk by taking regular exercise, eating a low fat diet and not smoking. The combination of nature and nurture determines our health.

► Cycling is an excellent form of exercise for all ages because it improves two aspects of fitness – muscle strength and stamina. Keeping fit can improve a person's health by helping to combat the possible tendency of certain genes, if present, to cause illnesses such as heart disease.

Gene therapy

Imagine if a car engine would not run because it had a faulty part. The simplest way to fix it would be to open the bonnet and put in a replacement. This is basically how gene therapy works. We have seen already that diseases such as haemophilia, cystic fibrosis and PKU are caused by a single faulty gene. Gene therapy aims to pinpoint the faulty gene and replace it with a normal, healthy gene in order to treat the illness. It is important to realize, however, that gene therapy is still in its early, experimental stages and does not, as yet, promise miracle cures.

Faulty genes

The first step in gene therapy is to spot the faulty gene. In the past, this was like looking for a needle in a haystack. But today, with several genetic diseases, scientists can pinpoint which gene is causing problems. New tools, such as DNA microarrays or DNA chips (shown on page 49) may one day help us understand still more diseases. The idea is that once the faulty gene is identified, it can be replaced by a normal gene. This will produce the right protein, usually an enzyme, to make cells work normally, and get rid of the disease. How do we get working genes into someone's body? Let's have a look at a specific example.

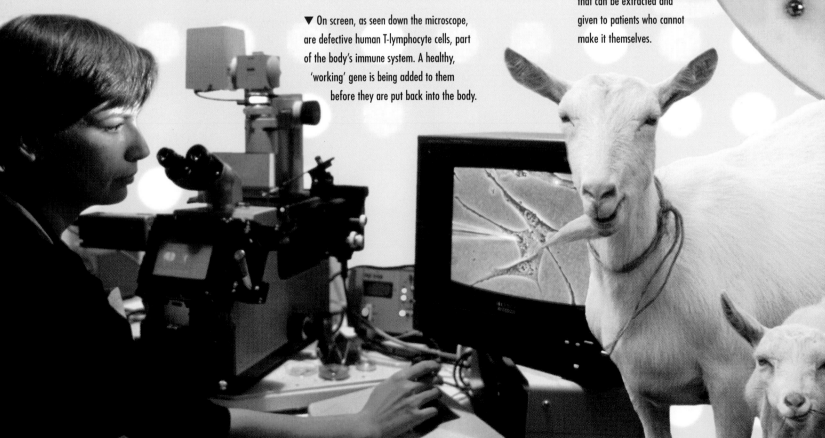

▼ These goats may look normal, but they have been genetically modified so that their milk produces a human protein that can be extracted and given to patients who cannot make it themselves.

▼ On screen, as seen down the microscope, are defective human T-lymphocyte cells, part of the body's immune system. A healthy, 'working' gene is being added to them before they are put back into the body.

Gene replacement

Severe combined immunodeficiency disease (SCID) is caused by a single gene mutation. Children with SCID have to be kept in isolation, often inside a special protective 'bubble'. This is because their immune systems (see pages 52–53) do not work properly and they could easily become very ill. In a few cases, doctors have treated SCID with gene therapy. First, they take cells from a patient's bone marrow. This is where cells called lymphocytes, which defend the body against germs, are made. They then use a specially modified virus (which invades cells) to carry a normal version of the faulty gene into the bone marrow cells. Back inside the body, these cells multiply and produce normal lymphocytes that can fight infection. Some children have begun to lead a normal, healthy life as a result.

Protein drugs

Gene therapy, like that used to treat SCID, is far from perfect. Scientists have a long way to go before it is a common treatment. In the meantime, some scientists are investigating how proteins – the products of genes – can be used to treat diseases. If a gene is faulty, we can treat the problem by finding another way to make sure the body gets the protein that gene would make if it worked properly. The goats on the left have been genetically modified to produce in their milk a protein called factor VIII, which can be used to treat people with haemophilia (see pages 32–33).

▲ Rhys Evans, seen here playing normally, was the first child in the UK to be treated successfully for SCID using gene therapy, at Great Ormond Street Hospital, London, England. Gene therapy was used to correct a gene defect that prevented his immune system from working properly.

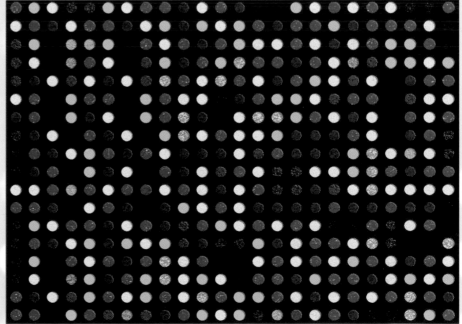

▶ This DNA microarray is a tool that allows scientists to compare how genes are working in a well person and in a person with a specific disease. Each dot shows scientists how a specific known gene is working in the two samples. They can see which genes are working differently from normal and use this information to find out more about the disease.

Perfect copies

When humans, and most other animals, reproduce, they do so sexually. A father's sperm and a mother's egg meet at fertilization, their chromosomes combine, and the offspring develops using an instruction set made of a mix of DNA from each parent. But some living things can reproduce asexually – that is, without sex. Take the Mexican hat plant. Like many other plants, it can simply bud off new offspring without the need for two parents. The plantlets are perfect copies of their 'parent', with identical genes, and are called clones. But if plants can produce clones of themselves, can we do the same?

▲ Along the edge of the leaf of this Mexican hat plant are miniature plantlets that will one day drop off and grow into new plants. These plantlets are clones. All of them share exactly the same DNA as the parent plant.

Cloning animals?

Animal clones can happen naturally, too. Identical twins (see pages 22–23) have identical DNA, and are natural clones. Some animals can reproduce asexually as well. Greenfly, for example, can reproduce either sexually or by the female giving birth to clones of herself. But what if we could make a perfect copy of an adult animal by cloning one of its cells? Think how useful this would be. If a cow was an excellent milk producer, we could make clones of her, with identical genes, that would also provide lots of milk. Or if we had successfully produced a GM animal, such as a goat, to produce useful medicines, that goat could be cloned to form a flock of identical, drug-making goats. This aim seemed impossible until 1996, when a cloned sheep called Dolly was born.

Making Dolly

How was Dolly produced? In a technique called nuclear transfer, scientists took cells from the udder of a six-year-old ewe (female sheep). The ewe they used was from a breed of sheep called the Finn Dorset. They also took some eggs from a ewe belonging to a different breed, the Scottish Blackface. Then they removed the nucleus from a Scottish Blackface egg and injected the 'empty' egg with the nucleus from a Finn Dorset udder cell. An electric shock fused the nucleus with the egg's cytoplasm, and the new embryo was implanted into the uterus of a 'foster mother', another Scottish Blackface ewe. Later, this ewe gave birth to Dolly, a lamb genetically identical to the original Finn Dorset ewe.

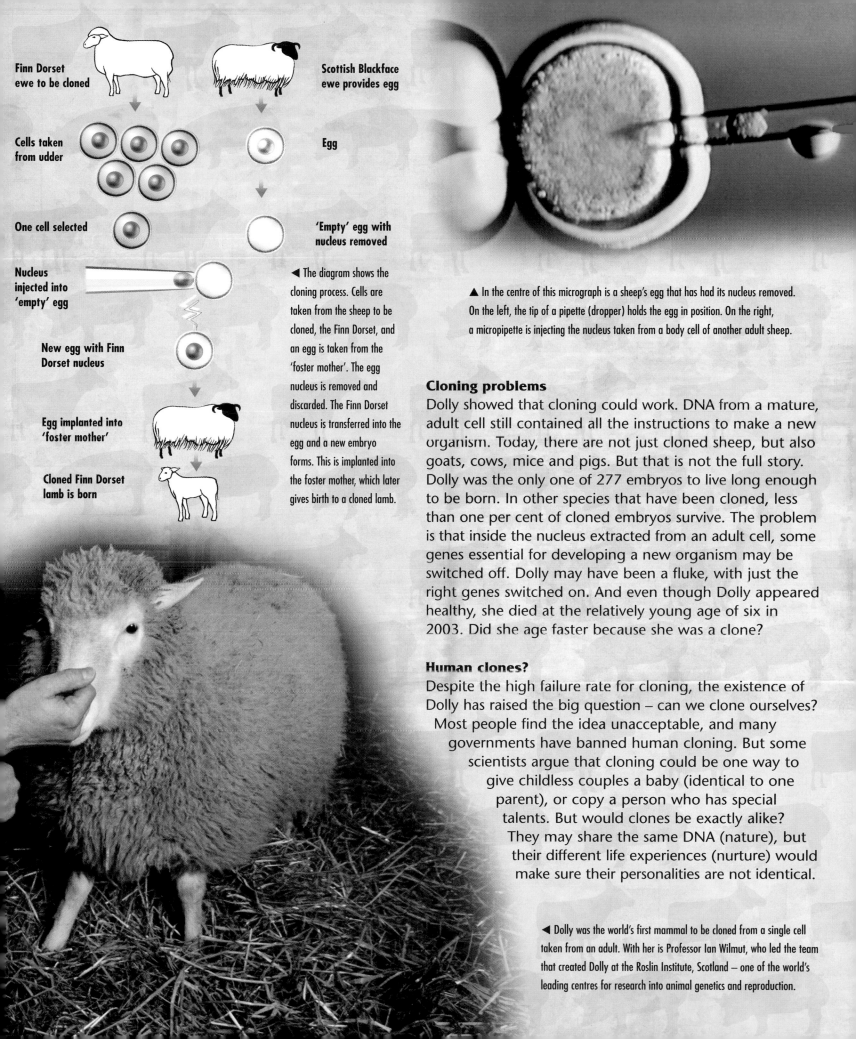

Finn Dorset ewe to be cloned

Cells taken from udder

One cell selected

Nucleus injected into 'empty' egg

New egg with Finn Dorset nucleus

Egg implanted into 'foster mother'

Cloned Finn Dorset lamb is born

Scottish Blackface ewe provides egg

Egg

'Empty' egg with nucleus removed

◀ The diagram shows the cloning process. Cells are taken from the sheep to be cloned, the Finn Dorset, and an egg is taken from the 'foster mother'. The egg nucleus is removed and discarded. The Finn Dorset nucleus is transferred into the egg and a new embryo forms. This is implanted into the foster mother, which later gives birth to a cloned lamb.

▲ In the centre of this micrograph is a sheep's egg that has had its nucleus removed. On the left, the tip of a pipette (dropper) holds the egg in position. On the right, a micropipette is injecting the nucleus taken from a body cell of another adult sheep.

Cloning problems

Dolly showed that cloning could work. DNA from a mature, adult cell still contained all the instructions to make a new organism. Today, there are not just cloned sheep, but also goats, cows, mice and pigs. But that is not the full story. Dolly was the only one of 277 embryos to live long enough to be born. In other species that have been cloned, less than one per cent of cloned embryos survive. The problem is that inside the nucleus extracted from an adult cell, some genes essential for developing a new organism may be switched off. Dolly may have been a fluke, with just the right genes switched on. And even though Dolly appeared healthy, she died at the relatively young age of six in 2003. Did she age faster because she was a clone?

Human clones?

Despite the high failure rate for cloning, the existence of Dolly has raised the big question – can we clone ourselves? Most people find the idea unacceptable, and many governments have banned human cloning. But some scientists argue that cloning could be one way to give childless couples a baby (identical to one parent), or copy a person who has special talents. But would clones be exactly alike? They may share the same DNA (nature), but their different life experiences (nurture) would make sure their personalities are not identical.

◀ Dolly was the world's first mammal to be cloned from a single cell taken from an adult. With her is Professor Ian Wilmut, who led the team that created Dolly at the Roslin Institute, Scotland — one of the world's leading centres for research into animal genetics and reproduction.

Spare parts

In 1967, the world's first successful heart transplant took place. One person's damaged heart was replaced by a healthy donor heart from another person. A major problem with transplants, however, is that the body rejects foreign organs, and patients only survive if they take anti-rejection drugs for the rest of their lives. Today, doctors want to use genetic technology in new kinds of treatments for a variety of serious illnesses. In theory, this could lead to transplants where there is no risk of rejection.

Risk of rejection

Our bodies are always at risk of invasion by bacteria, viruses, and other germs that cause diseases. We have a sophisticated defence system, though – our immune system – that destroys invaders. Cells such as macrophages (shown below), and special chemicals called antibodies, disable and destroy anything foreign. Unfortunately, this means they destroy any cells transplanted into the body from another person. This is because all cells carry on their surface tiny markers – determined by their genes – that identify cells as either 'self' or 'foreign'. The immune system ignores 'self' cells, but acts immediately to destroy 'foreign' ones.

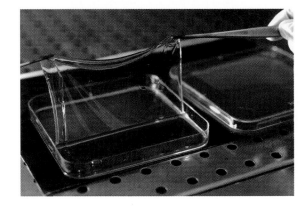

▲ Skin can be grown artificially so it can be used to graft onto a person's body, for example if his or her skin has been badly burned. If skin could be cloned from the patient's own cells it would not be rejected.

Stem cells

There are over 200 different kinds of cell in the human body. Stem cells are special because they can develop into just about every other cell type in the body. This means they could be transplanted into a patient to replace tissue that has been damaged by illness or accident. The 'best' stem cells come from a human embryo that is just a few days old. But using embryos for this purpose is not acceptable to many people. Also, like donor organs, they are a 'foreign' source and would be rejected by the body.

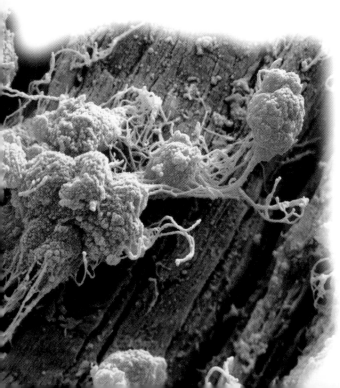

◀ Macrophages (white) are cells that form part of the body's defence force. They are attacking threads (green) that have been used to stitch a wound together. The macrophages recognize the threads as being 'foreign'.

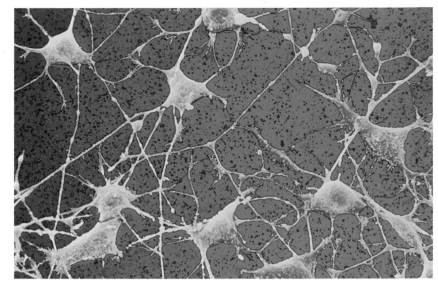

► These are just some of the 100 billion neurons in the human brain. Each one can have hundreds or thousands of links with other neurons, forming a complex communication network that allows us to see, hear and feel, and controls all of our movements. Brain neurons, as well as those in the spinal cord (which extends from the brain down the back), cannot be replaced once they die. One day, cloning might provide a way of growing new brain cells.

Cloning to heal

Cloning (see pages 50–51) would be a way to avoid the problem of rejection. Scientists would take a cell from the person who needs to be treated, insert its nucleus into an 'empty' human egg cell, then let this egg divide into a mass of stem cells. This is called 'therapeutic' cloning because it makes just a few stem cells rather than a whole person ('therapeutic' means healing). These could be transplanted back into the patient without risk of rejection, because they would carry his or her genes. Imagine, for example, if a person had Parkinson's disease. This happens when neurons (nerve cells) in part of the brain start to die, causing a person to lose the ability to move properly. It may be that, one day, 'self' stem cells could be injected into the brain to replace the missing neurons.

▲ This is a human embryo just three days after fertilization. The fertilized egg has divided to produce a ball of eight cells — stem cells. At this stage, the cells have not started to develop into different types of cell, and have the potential to grow into any type.

Superman's fight

In 1995, actor Christopher Reeve was thrown from his horse, damaging his spinal cord so he could no longer feel or move his body below the neck. Before his death in 2004, he campaigned for stem-cell research. He believed that stem cells could, one day, be used to form new neurons – the cells found in the spinal cord – that would repair spinal damage. He understood that some people object to using cells from embryos that are then discarded. But researchers are finding that in future it may be possible to re-program adult cells to behave in the same way as stem cells do now.

► American film actor Christopher Reeve, famous for his role in the *Superman* films, was paralyzed from the neck downwards following a riding accident in 1995. Before his death, he set up a foundation that continues to fund research into treating paralysis.

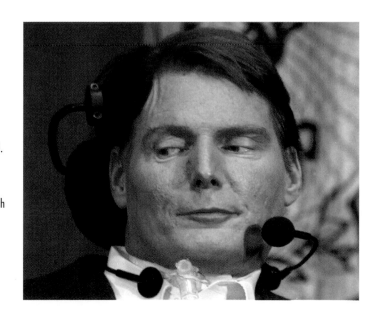

Extinct and endangered

Just think about these frightening figures. It is thought that around 100 animal species become extinct (die out) every day. Many other animals, including the giant panda and the chimpanzee, are referred to as endangered, because they are at risk of extinction. Over a quarter of all plant species are also on the endangered list and may have vanished in 50 years' time. Usually, they are extinct or endangered because we humans are destroying their natural habitats. Remarkably, some scientists think that they can use DNA technology, including cloning, to save endangered species – or even, perhaps, use DNA to bring extinct species back to life.

▲ Although it looks as though it died just minutes ago, this blood-sucking insect, fossilized in amber, is millions of years old. Living at the same time as dinosaurs, the insect became trapped in sticky resin that oozed out of an ancient pine tree and hardened to form its clear, amber prison.

Return of the dinosaurs?

After being extinct for 65 million years, dinosaurs were brought back to life – although only in the fictional world of the film *Jurassic Park*. How? By taking fossilized biting insects that fed on dinosaur blood, extracting DNA from the dinosaur blood cells inside them, and using it as an instruction set to rebuild dinosaurs. Could this work in real life? The answer seems to be 'No'. After so many millions of years, little if any of the dinosaur DNA would remain. However, scientists in Australia want to clone a thylacine – a wolf-like species that became extinct in 1936 – using DNA taken from a preserved specimen.

▼ This giant panda is one of only an estimated 1,000 to 2,000 left in their natural habitat, the mountainous bamboo forests of southwest China. To help in the effort to save this endangered species, scientists plan to produce a cloned giant panda, using an American black bear as its 'foster mother'.

▲ In this scene from Steven Spielberg's 1993 film *Jurassic Park*, astonished – and soon-to-be-terrified – visitors are touring a very unusual wildlife park. It is unusual because it is populated by dinosaurs recreated from ancient DNA. But could extinct animals really be brought back from the dead?

Saved by cloning?

It is easier to help endangered animals than revive extinct ones, because the endangered ones are still alive. One way of doing so is by cloning, using the same method that created Dolly the sheep (see pages 50–51). Scientists take a cell from the rare animal, fuse it with an 'empty' egg from a related but much more common species, and then let it develop inside the uterus of a female of that species. This has already been done with a gaur, a rare Asian type of cattle, born after developing inside a domestic cow.

◀ Soaring high in the sky in search of dead animals to feed on, this California condor, a type of vulture, is the largest bird in North America. It is also one of the most endangered species on earth.

◀ Dr Oliver Ryder, head of genetics at the Zoological Society of San Diego, California, USA, is holding a DNA 'map' that compares the genetic fingerprints of several California condors and shows how closely related they are. This is an important part of condor conservation.

Captive breeding

If a species is facing extinction, why not capture the remaining animals and breed them in a zoo? This is what happened when numbers of the California condor fell to just 27 birds in the mid-1980s. Thanks to a captive breeding programme, by 2006 there were more than 270 California condors, 125 of which had been released back into the wild. DNA fingerprinting played a vital role by identifying closely-related condors. This is important because if close relatives breed together, they are more likely to produce offspring with a serious inherited problem.

▶ The animal species shown here, including the African elephant, gorilla, tiger and golden lion tamarin, are just a sample of those that risk extinction. This is not to mention the many tropical forest plants and animals that are destroyed before they can even be identified.

Frozen zoos

Another way to save threatened species could be the establishment of 'frozen zoos', like the one already set up in San Diego, USA. Here, cells from thousands of endangered species are deep frozen. If an animal becomes extinct, its cells might one day be unfrozen and used for cloning in order to bring that species back to life. But many people think that using DNA technology to help endangered species diverts us from the real problem. They feel we need to protect and restore habitats to stop species becoming endangered in the first place.

Predicting the future

In 50 years, we have come from knowing nothing about DNA to being able to sequence the DNA in the entire human genome. So, what predictions can we make about the future? Scientists will certainly find themselves occupied with the task of identifying specific genes in the genome and finding out what proteins these genes produce. But other things are more uncertain. Will we all know our own genomes and therefore our genetic fate? Will genetic modification improve the health of everyone? And will we be able to choose what our children look like? Only time will tell.

▶ This futuristic ID card carries information, such as a photograph, fingerprint and scan of the iris, that are familiar to us now. But future technology might allow each person's genome to be sequenced, scanned and recorded on a card like this.

Personal profile

By 2025, it should be possible to carry out a complete genome sequencing in just hours. This could mean that, as a matter of routine, every newborn baby would be given a complete genetic profile. Just after birth, a blood sample would be taken, DNA extracted and sequenced, and the gene information recorded and transferred to an ID card. This genetic information could be used by doctors to predict if someone might develop a condition, such as heart disease, in the future, so they could adopt measures, such as a healthier lifestyle, to help prevent it. But there is a real fear that if a person's gene 'problems' are known, he or she could find it difficult to get work, or insurance, for fear that he or she will probably get certain diseases.

▶ Embedded in the ID card's chip is a list of genes, including those that might indicate the risk of certain diseases. The card could be read by a doctor, using a computer, and so it is a step up from the ID bracelets people with certain medical conditions carry today. It could also be read by the police, or anyone else authorized to use the information. Some people might object to people having access to this information about them. But could we all be carrying cards like this in the future?

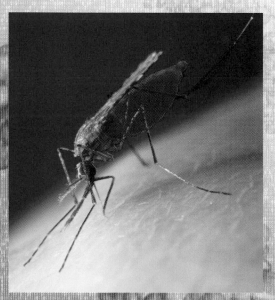

◀ This is a female *Anopheles* mosquito, an insect that spreads the deadly disease malaria by biting into human skin, as it is doing here, and sucking blood. Scientists are working to produce GM mosquitoes that are unable to pass on the disease. Could this make a difference to the spread of malaria around the world?

Better treatment

One great hope for the future is for better, more precise, treatment of illnesses. We have already seen the possibility of using gene therapy – inserting genes to replace those that are defective (see pages 48–49). This will probably take some time to perfect, but a more practical and immediate prospect is that of customizing drugs. At the moment, many drugs are chemicals that happen to treat certain diseases, often without scientists knowing exactly why. Knowledge of the human genome should allow scientists to create drugs that treat a disease specifically by changing the way a gene works. And since each person's genes affect how they react to a particular drug, different versions of drugs could be produced to match an individual's genetic make-up.

Genes at work

The quickest and cheapest way to produce these drugs, and other products, would be to use genetically modified (GM) organisms (see pages 44–45). A vaccine to protect against measles could be produced inside GM fruit, which would then be eaten by children, avoiding the need for injections. GM mosquitoes that are modified so that they do not carry the deadly malarial parasite could be released into the wild, where they would breed with 'normal' mosquitoes. Eventually, perhaps, they would cause malaria to be wiped out. It is an attractive thought. GM bacteria could even be developed that could clean up nuclear waste sites and remove a hazard that would otherwise last for thousands of years.

Designer babies?

In future, could humans be able to 'design' their own children? It is already possible to 'screen' an embryo, before it develops into a baby, to check that it is free of certain gene mutations. In 20 years' time, it might be possible to select an embryo with, say, genes for being tall. In 40 years' time, it might even be possible to modify an embryo's genome to introduce specific characteristics such as ability at maths or longer life. Some people feel that wiping out diseases and giving children a head start in life is a good thing. Others believe that people are more than just their genes, and we should leave the genetic make-up of our children to nature.

SUMMARY OF CHAPTER 3: GENETIC TECHNOLOGY

Applying the knowledge
The practical use of DNA and genes, called genetic technology or gene science, is one of the fastest growing areas of scientific research. But what is it? How will it affect us? Does everyone agree with it? What does the future hold? We have addressed these questions in Chapter 3.

Modifying the message
Scientists have also been able to make use of the fact that DNA is the same, and works the same way, in all living things. This makes genetic engineering possible. Genetic engineering involves transferring a 'useful' gene from one species into another species to produce a particular beneficial feature. Modifying the DNA message in this way may also, one day, provide a cure for some inherited diseases in the form of gene therapy, which replaces a faulty gene with a healthy one.

Detective work
Being able to identify people by small differences in their DNA has allowed both police and scientists to do some detective work. Police can call on forensic scientists to prepare a DNA fingerprint from cells found at a crime scene to help them prove a suspect's guilt or innocence. Scientists have used DNA evidence to trace the spread of humans from Africa, where they first evolved, around the world. They have also used DNA evidence to examine ancient remains, including human mummies and fossilized animals.

Making copies
Scientists are now able, with some difficulty, to make perfect copies, or clones, of mammals such as sheep. This has all sorts of implications. It is already possible to make herds of identical animals genetically engineered to produce drugs. Cloning may also allow scientists to copy the few remaining individuals of an endangered species so that they do not become extinct. And perhaps it may also allow them to make special cells that would replace diseased tissues in the body.

Go further...

Discover facts about cloning, genetic engineering and lots more at:
http://ology.amnh.org/genetics/index.html

Find out about genetic technology with the help of Tiki the Penguin at:
http://tiki.oneworld.net/genetics/GE12.html

Find out about research into gene therapy and the Jeans for Genes charity at:
www.jeansforgenes.com/about/researchandsupport/

Forensic scientist
Analyzes evidence from crime scenes to help police with finding criminals.

Veterinary scientist
Medically examines and treats animals, and researches into their health.

Conservationist
Studies animals and plants at risk of extinction, and ways to save them.

Genetic counsellor
Advises couples on the possibility of their having a child with an inherited disease.

Biomedical scientist
Applies science to medicine, such as in the use of stem cell research.

To find out more about genetic technology, visit the American Museum of Natural History:
www.amnh.org/museum
Central Park and 79th Street, New York City NY, USA
T: 001 (212) 769 5100

To observe the similarities between animal groups for yourself and find out about rare species, take a trip to a zoo, such as London Zoo or Edinburgh Zoo:
www.londonzoo.org
Regent's Park,
London NW1 4RY
T: 020 7722 3333
www.edinburghzoo.org.uk
Murrayfield,
Edinburgh EH12 6TS
T: 0131 334 9171

Glossary

allele
One of two or more alternative versions of the same gene.

amino acid
One of 20 chemical compounds that are the building blocks of proteins.

ancestor
A relative that lived hundreds or thousands of years ago.

atom
A tiny particle of an element, such as carbon, from which all matter is made.

bacterium (plural bacteria)
One of a group of simple, single-celled organisms, some of which cause diseases in humans.

base
One of four chemical substances – adenine (A), cytosine (C), guanine (G) and thymine (T) – that form the 'letters' in DNA.

blood group
One of four 'types' of blood – A, B, AB or O – determined by markers on red blood cells. A person's blood group is wholly controlled by genes.

cell
One of the tiny living units from which organisms are made.

cell membrane
The thin, protective membrane that surrounds a cell.

characteristic
A feature, such as blue eyes, shown by a human or other organism.

chromosome
One of the 46 thread-like structures composed of DNA and protein, found inside the nucleus of most human cells.

cloning
Making an identical copy of a living organism, with the same DNA.

code
A system used to translate a message in one language into a message in another. Cells use the genetic code to convert DNA's sequence of bases into a sequence of amino acids.

codon
Groups of three bases that form the 'words' that make up the instructions in genes.

competition
The struggle between living things for natural resources.

component
One of the parts from which something is made. DNA's components are phosphate, deoxyribose and the bases A, C, G and T.

cytoplasm
The thick fluid that forms most of the inside of a cell.

determine
To decide or fix.

development
Increase in complexity that occurs as a living organism grows. A human fertilized egg, for example, develops from a ball of identical cells into a foetus with a head, arms, legs and

hundreds of different types of cells.

DNA (Deoxyribonucleic acid)
The chemical found in the nucleus of a cell that makes up chromosomes and genes.

DNA fingerprint
A sample of DNA taken from a person, and broken up to form a pattern that is unique to that person.

dominant
Describes an allele or gene that produces a feature in an organism.

double helix
The name given to the twin strands that spiral around each other in a DNA molecule.

draft
An outline version of something.

ECG (Electrocardiogram)
A recording of the electrical signals that pass through the heart during each heartbeat.

egg
A female sex cell, also called an ovum.

embryo
The name given to an unborn child during the first eight weeks after fertilization.

endangered
Describes an animal or plant that is at risk of becoming extinct, or dying out.

environment
A living thing's surroundings, and everything in them.

enzyme
A type of protein found in the body, that greatly speeds up the rate of chemical reactions inside and outside cells.

evolution
The gradual change of living organisms over time.

extinct
Describes a species of living organism that has died out and disappeared. Dinosaurs, for example, are extinct.

fertility
The ability of living things to have offspring. Sometimes, if people are finding it difficult to have children, they have treatment to improve their fertility.

fertilization
The joining together of an egg and sperm to produce a new living organism. It is at fertilization that each individual's unique package of chromosomes, with their genes, is produced.

foetus
The name given to an unborn child from the ninth week after fertilization until birth.

fossilized
Describes the remains of a living organism that have been preserved over many years.

gene
One of the instructions carried on the DNA within chromosomes.

generation
Level of relationship, such as parents, which belong to one generation, and offspring, which belong to the next.

genetic
Describes something to do with genes and inheritance.

genetic engineering
Artificial change made to the genes or DNA of a living organism.

genome
A complete set of the genes found in a living organism. The human genome consists of all the genes in one of the two sets of chromosomes in each body cell.

GM organism
An organism whose genes have been altered, or engineered, to change a specific feature or features. GM stands for genetically modified.

habitat
Place where an animal or plant lives.

haemophilia
An inherited disease in which normal blood clotting does not occur.

Human Genome Project
Research programme to discover the sequence of bases in human DNA and eventually identify all the genes in the human genome.

immune system
The system in the body that protects the body from infection by bacteria and other germs. It is made up of a collection of cells including lymphocytes and macrophages.

inheritance
The transmission, or passing on, of features controlled by genes from both parents to their offspring.

'junk' DNA
Long, repeated sections of DNA, found between and within genes, that appear to have no role.

locus
Position on matching maternal and paternal chromosomes at which alleles of the same gene are found.

maternal
Describes something belonging to, or coming from, the mother.

meiosis
The type of cell division that produces sex cells – such as sperm and eggs – that contain a single set of chromosomes.

melanin
A brown pigment (colouring) which gives skin its colour. The more melanin that is present, the darker the colour.

micrograph
A photograph taken with the aid of a microscope.

microscope
An instrument used to magnify very small objects.

mitochondria (singular mitochondrion)
Tiny structures in cells that release energy for cell activities. They also contain their own type of DNA, mitochondrial DNA (mtDNA).

mitosis
The type of cell division involved in growth and repair that produces two 'daughter' cells that are genetically identical to their 'parent'.

molecule
A chemical unit, such as DNA, made up of two or more atoms.

mutation
A change in the base sequence of DNA, caused by an error in copying or some other factor. A mutation may be passed on to offspring.

natural selection
The process that favours organisms best

adapted to their surroundings, and therefore more likely to survive, breed and pass on their favourable genes.

nature
In genetics, the influence of genes on the features of an organism. Nature in this context is often compared with 'nurture'.

neuron
A nerve cell – the basic unit of the nervous system including the brain.

nucleotide
One of the building blocks of DNA, made up of phosphate, deoxyribose and a base – A, C, G or T.

nucleus (plural nuclei)
The control centre of a cell, which contains the chromosomes.

nurture
The influence of environment – where and how someone or something lives – on the features of an organism. Often compared with 'nature'.

offspring
The child or descendant of parents or a parent.

organism
A living thing, such as an animal (including humans) or plant.

ovaries
The reproductive organs in females that produce eggs.

paternal
Describes something belonging to, or coming from, the father.

physiotherapy
Use of exercise and massage to treat various illnesses and injuries.

PKU (Phenylketonuria)
An inherited disorder in which the amino acid phenylalanine builds up in the bloodstream.

placenta
The organ found in the uterus during pregnancy through which the growing foetus receives food and oxygen.

pollination
In plants, transfer of pollen, containing the male sex cell, to the female part of a flower, to allow fertilization to take place.

pore
A hole or opening, for example in the membrane around the nucleus.

protein
One of a group of chemical substances that build and run cells. Proteins are built of amino acids using instructions encoded in genes.

radiation
Rays given off by radioactive materials, which may cause gene mutation.

recessive
Describes an allele, or gene, that does not usually produce a feature in an organism because it is masked by a dominant allele. A recessive allele will produce a feature only if the dominant allele is not also present.

replication
Making an exact copy of itself, as in a DNA molecule replicating to make two new identical copies.

reproductive system
The body system, either male or female, that plays a part in producing children. A body system is made up of several organs which work together to do a certain job.

ribosome
A structure inside the cell on which proteins are made.

RNA (Ribonucleic acid)
A chemical substance similar to but smaller than DNA, and with one strand instead of two, that plays a key role in protein synthesis.

sex cells
The cells such as sperm and eggs that are involved in sexual reproduction.

species
A group of similar living things, such as humans, that can breed together and produce offspring.

stem cells
Cells that can grow into all, or most, types of body cells.

supercoil
A coil within a coil. Each chromosome is made of a long DNA molecule tightly coiled in a supercoil.

testes
The reproductive organs in males that produce sperm.

tissue
A group of the same, or similar, types of cells, such as muscle cells, that co-operate to carry out a specific function.

transcription
The copying of a section of DNA (a gene) into messenger RNA. Transcription is the first phase of protein synthesis.

translation
The conversion of the message carried by messenger RNA using the genetic code into a sequence of amino acids. Translation is the second phase of protein synthesis.

transplant
The replacement of a diseased tissue or organ by healthy tissue or organ taken from another person.

twin
One of a pair of children produced during the same pregnancy.

uterus
The part of the female reproductive system in which the baby grows and develops during pregnancy. It is also called the womb.

vitamin
One of a group of chemical substances which the body needs in small amounts in food in order to stay healthy.

X-ray
The form of radiation used to reveal bones and other body organs. It was also used to help work out the structure of the DNA molecule.

Index

Acknowledgements

The publisher would like to thank the following for permission to reproduce their material. Every care has been taken to trace copyright holders. However, if there have been unintentional omissions or failure to trace copyright holders, we apologize and will, if informed, endeavour to make corrections in any future edition.

Key: *b* = bottom, *c* = centre, *l* = left, *r* = right, *t* = top

Cover Science Photo Library (SPL)/James King-Holmes; 1 SPL; 2–3 SPL; 4 SPL; 7 Getty Images; 10*tr* SPL; 10*bl* Art Archive; 11*br* Ardea; 12*tr* SPL; 12*bl* SPL; 14–15*t* SPL; 15*cl* SPL; 15*br* SPL; 16*br* Getty Images; 17*tl* SPL; 17*tr* SPL; 17*br* SPL; 18*tl* SPL; 18–19 Getty Images; 19*br* SPL; 20*tl* SPL; 20*cr* Corbis; 20*b* Corbis; 20–21*b* Getty Images; 21*tr* Corbis; 21*cl* Corbis; 21*b* Corbis; 22*tr* Corbis; 22*bl* SPL; 23*tr* SPL; 23*bl* PA Photos; 24 SPL; 25 SPL; 26*bl* ROSALIND FRANKLIN; 26*cr* SPL; 26–27 SPL; 27*br* SPL; 28*br* SPL; 31*tc* SPL; 31*tr* SPL; 31*cr* SPL; 32*tl* SPL; 32*cl* SPL; 32–33*b* Corbis; 33*c* Hulton Getty; 34*l* SPL; 34*r* SPL; 35*tl* SPL; 35*tr* SPL; 35*br* SPL; 36*tl* SPL; 36*br* Natural History Picture Agency (NHPA); 37*tl* SPL; 37*tr* SPL; 37*bl* NHPA; 38 SPL; 39 SPL; 41*cl* SPL; 41*br* ImagingBody, Edinburgh; 42*b* Corbis; 43*tl* SPL; 43*tc* Associated Press; 43*tr* Corbis; 43*cr* Rex Features; 44*tl* SPL; 44*bl* Corbis; 44*br* Corbis; 44–45 SPL; 45*tr* Corbis; 45*br* Corbis; 46*tl* SPL; 46*cl* Corbis; 46*br* Corbis; 47*tr* Corbis; 47*b* Corbis; 48*bl* SPL; 48*br* Getty Images; 49*tl* PA Photos; 49*br* SPL; 50*tl* Oxford Scientific Films; 50–51 Corbis; 51*t* SPL; 52*cl* SPL; 52*bl* SPL; 53*tr* SPL; 53*cr* SPL; 53*br* Rex Features; 54*tl* SPL; 54*cr* Corbis; 54*bl* Corbis; 55*tl* SPL; 55*tr* Associated Press; 56 SPL; 59*tl* SPL; 59*b* SPL; 64*br* Ardea.

Commissioned photography on pages 8–9 and 41 by Andy Crawford. Thank you to models Carron Brown, Primrose Burton, Elaine Chon-Baker, Eleanor Davis, Mike Davis and Philip Newton.

The publisher would like to thank the following illustrators:
Mark Bristow 33; Mike Buckley *cover*; Peter Bull 18; Sam Combes 50–51 (background); Tom Connell 28–29, 30–31; Mark Preston 56–57; Sebastien Quigley (Linden Artists) 8–9, 11, 13, 14, 19, 40–41, 51 (main illustration), 52–53; Steve Weston (Linden Artists) 23.

The author would like to thank Catherine Brereton for her enthusiasm and creativity, Peter Clayman for his excellent designs, and other members of the Kingfisher team for their hard work.